Where Family and Finance Meet

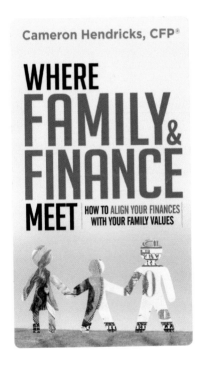

WHERE FAMILY AND FINANCE MEET

HOW TO ALIGN YOUR FINANCES
WITH YOUR FAMILY VALUES

Cameron Hendricks

ISBN: 0998821454
ISBN 13: 9780998821450
Library of Congress Control Number: 2017905249
Cameron Hendricks, Holly Springs, NC

TABLE OF CONTENTS

INTRODUCTION

We all belong to a family of some kind. This may be the traditional family tree including parents, siblings, cousins, etc., or it could be organizations or communities that you associate yourself with. This could be your workplace family, church family, or close neighbors.

These "family" members are the people you most often associate with, and you go to them whenever you seek advice or direction for challenges that you face. You trust them and want to hear their opinions or thoughts on various subjects, from recipes or home repair to finances and relational issues.

They also influence your decisions and are often the basis for why you make certain decisions, even if you have not directly consulted them on the issue. I'll bet that if you tracked your time and money spent for the rest of the year, you would see that the findings reflect your association to certain family groups. That vacation you took last summer—the destination was recommended by a family member. The steakhouse you frequent weekly—recommended by a family member. The season tickets for your alma mater's football team reflect the time you enjoy spending on Saturdays with your alumni family. The increased Christmas gifts because of your new niece or nephew or grandchild. The charitable gifts you make to a cause you care deeply about. The expensive obedience lessons for your "special" dog. All of these things reveal the impact your various families have on your decision making.

Okay, fine—I have to admit, the "special" dog example comes from my own personal experience and was actually my inspiration to start writing this book. You see, my wife and I have only one child, and he is of the four-legged variety. We got Charlie, a black Lab, when he was six weeks old, the year we got married. Five years later, he is an important part of our family, and we enjoy him—sometimes a little too much! He has always been a little on the wild and crazy side and has had numerous health and social issues. While these have been difficult to deal with at times, emotionally and financially, since he is a member of our family, we have committed to loving him and taking care of his needs.

After a repeated occurrence of behavioral issues, we decided it was time to take action. We began researching various long-term "board and train" programs throughout North Carolina, in which he could get some special one-on-one time with a trainer to become more socialized and obedient. We ended up choosing a trainer in Rockingham, North Carolina, where Charlie spent three weeks going through exhausting training, in the hope that he would improve as a family pet.

At the end of the three-week program, my wife and I made the one-and-a-half-hour drive down to Rockingham from Holly Springs, North Carolina, and upon pulling into the driveway, we could hear Charlie whimpering in excitement as his tail wagged uncontrollably. It made us so relieved to see that he missed us, and we immediately greeted him as he licked our faces and jumped around in circles, trying to demonstrate his newly learned skills but still wanting to show his love and affection for us. We spent a few hours going over his obedience training so that we could maintain his new skills after we brought him home. When it was time to leave, we loaded him in the car and weren't even to the end of the driveway before he was snoring in the backseat, as this was probably one of the first times he'd been able to truly relax during the entire three-week period.

During the drive home, as my wife and I rehashed the training session, we validated the reason for sending Charlie to this extended board and train. We discussed how we were looking forward to going on walks in our neighborhood or having friends over for dinner without having to worry about how our dog would behave. Overall, we just wanted our dog, and therefore our family, to be the best that it could be.

It dawned on me then that our "families" are some of the top reasons for why we make the decisions we make. Family was the reason we sent our dog to a stranger for three weeks at a cost that we were a little uncomfortable paying. Was it worth it in the end? Only time will answer that question, but I do know that I would make the same decision again.

As my wife drifted off for a short car nap on our way back north on US 1 through central North Carolina, I began to think of examples of other people I had seen who made decisions or had desires based on their families. During my time as a financial planner, I've had the unique experience of learning what makes my clients tick. I learn what gets them excited and passionate about their desire to improve their financial situation. Why they want to retire a few years early; why they want to contribute to a 529 college savings plan; why they want to make sure their estate documents are in order; why they want to make sure they make charitable contributions annually; why they have trouble keeping their lifestyle expenses in line with the targets set forth in their financial plans.

As I thought about all this, I asked myself, what was the overwhelming, common theme I kept reverting back to? Family.

I eagerly waited for my wife to wake up, then delivered this new book idea to her. Anticipating her feedback, I prefaced the idea with a warning that this was going to come out of left field.

"You may think I'm crazy," I said, "but I had an idea, and I want to run with it. What do you think about me writing a book?"

As we sat at a stoplight in Pinehurst, North Carolina, she blankly stared back at me, and I began babbling about my idea and why I was so excited about it. After a few more blank stares, she finally responded, "What would you write about?"

I explained that it would be related to finance, as I had enjoyed writing financial blog posts for my company's website. I then pointed to our sleeping dog in the back seat. With a puzzled look, she asked, "You're going to write a financial book about Charlie?"

As much as this first chapter may seem to be about my five-year-old black Lab, I responded "No. Family. I want to write a book about finances and how our financial decisions are influenced by our families."

In the coming chapters, I will discuss a variety of financial planning topics and how our families influence our thought processes behind decisions involving these topics. I will walk through scenarios I have experienced with clients, as well as personal examples in order to provide you, the reader, with a vision for your finances and how to align them with your family values. These are two areas of my life that I am passionate about, and I believe they are inextricably intertwined.

This book is for those who want to align their finances with their family values. These values are how you have shaped your life and your family's life. They, therefore, are the foundations that motivate your financial decisions. When your finances align with your family values, you are more likely to implement strategies to help you reflect these values, as they are the basis for how you want your family to live financially.

This book will show you how to make financial decisions that are both in-line with your values *and* financially sound. For example, your family may prioritize education planning, whether K–12 or undergraduate and graduate school. In the College Planning chapter, I will dive into ways you can save and pay for college. Or maybe you want your family to be generous with their giving but don't know the best way to do that. We will explore the most tax efficient ways to make charitable donations, as well as ways to give gifts to other members of your family such as your children or grandchildren.

Ultimately, I am going to walk you through how to grow your wealth so that you can utilize it for the good of your family and others you care about. From growing your wealth to ultimately passing it on to generations to come, this book is going to be the road map for individuals focused on their family finances.

CHAPTER 1

FAMILY & BUDGETING

Maybe "budgeting" isn't the right word, or maybe it's just not the word you want to hear. After all, countless articles and books have touched on this subject, mostly with a negative connotation. So it's not surprising that you may have some resistance to the topic, as you may have negative associations or experiences with budgeting.

What if I told you that budgeting means the exact opposite to me? Would you believe that budgeting doesn't have to be a negative, restricting, guilt-inducing experience? It may have taken me a little bit of time to believe that myself and even longer for my wife, but she'll give her side of the story in a minute.

So if budgeting doesn't mean restriction to me, then what does it mean? Well, to me, budgeting means freedom. That's right, I said *freedom*. Not freedom as in, I get to spend whatever I want with no rhyme or reason (that's just being irresponsible). What

I mean when I say freedom is that I am free to spend on certain items up until I hit a predetermined amount. How do I get that predetermined amount, you may ask? Well, it's a discussion that my wife and I have during our monthly budget meeting at the beginning of each month. We've been doing this for about two years now, and it has made a world of difference in our finances.

Thinking back to when we first got married and combined our finances, there was a lot of guilt in our spending and a lot of stress and arguing as a result. Every basketball game I bought a ticket for was used as ammo from my wife when I would question her about her latest Target purchase. On top of our usual spending, we were met with surprise expenses from her fourteen-year-old Ford Explorer (aka Dora the Explorer) as well as our new puppy Charlie, who, as I mentioned, had many health issues.

All of that guilt and at least most of the stress have since abated. You see, when we were first married and had arguments around our finances, we didn't have a plan. We didn't know how much we could spend on certain items without hindering our financial future.

Monthly Budget Meeting

So how did we get to this place of (nearly) stress-free, no-guilt spending? The answer is communication. This is not an easy, simple answer, as finances and communication are among the top sources of conflict between spouses.[1]

At first, we sat down on the Sunday night preceding each month and set a budget for various categories so that we would know how much we could spend over the course of the next month. The first few months were a little bit of trial and error, as items came up unexpectedly, or we got halfway through the month and essentially gave up on trying to stay within the budget.

After these first few months, we started to get the hang of the monthly budget and did a better job of preparing for those unexpected "one-off" expenses such as scheduled car repairs, a birthday present for a friend, or an annual trip to the eye doctor.

Why Budget?

Sticking to a budget is all well and good, but what is the true benefit of doing so? Here are the benefits of budgeting and how they may relate to your family.

1. Remember the "freeing" feeling that I mentioned budgeting has created for my family at the beginning of the chapter? That feeling has been huge in discussions between my wife and me about finances over the last few years. It has enabled us to

openly discuss our goals and objectives involving our finances and how we can accomplish them.

No longer are we building up tension over the latest trip to the grocery store or the extra fast food lunch with coworkers. As long as they fall within the preset budget target, it's all good!

2. "When setting up your budget, if saving and giving is at the bottom, then your budget is upside down." —Dave Ramsey.[2]

This quote has really stuck with me, and it is the way we set up our budget each month. The first thing we do each month is estimate our income and then delegate how much we want to "give" and "save" each month. Then we are free to spend what is left on various categories because we know we will still meet our saving and giving goals because that money was set aside *first.* If we flipped this and saved or gave what was left after our daily living expenses, then there would be very little or nothing left, hindering our longer-term goals and our ability to save for the future and give generously along the way.

3. The pastor at our church, JD Greear, has said a number of times to "look at what you spend your time and money on, and you will see what is truly important to you." This is another quote that has resonated with me over the years, and I have seen it in action in our family budget. Without the budget, we

can easily get trapped in spending more on unimportant items such as a spur-of-the-moment emotional purchase at the local boutique or a shiny new "toy" at the local hardware store.

However, with the budget, we can allocate money for what is truly important to us. So, if giving to your church or favorite charitable organization is important to you, then setting that money aside in your budget will help you accomplish this goal. Other areas where I think this works well are birthday presents to friends and family, sporting events that bring family together, and health-related expenses to maintain your overall well-being. If we allocate a portion of our budget to these items, then there is less money to spend on the things that are less important to us.

4. Monthly budgeting is focused on the short term but ultimately has long-term results. What I mean by this is that it may seem unnecessary to keep a tight budget when you know you have some savings in the bank, but maintaining a disciplined budget—where you are also saving a certain amount each month—allows you to save up for larger desired items or experiences, such as that week-long family vacation at the beach or even longer-term goals such as assisting with your children's college tuition. These larger items may seem insurmountable, but saving a little each month can really allow for these things to happen over time.

I want to take this opportunity to share some input from the point of view of someone who was initially resistant to and skeptical of budgeting: my wife, Abby.

Budgeting Insights from Abby

When my husband Cameron first suggested keeping a budget in the early years of our marriage, I was honestly extremely resistant. It was the first time as adults that we were both out of school and had full-time jobs, and I thought we could be carefree with our money for a while before buckling down. There would be plenty of time later to worry about that, and I thought a budget meant I would never be able to go shopping at Target or buy a new pair of shoes again!

Talking about our finances also stressed me out. While I knew that our income was sufficient to meet our everyday needs, I wasn't sure if it would be enough to cover big expenses like a new roof on our house or a down payment for a new car, both of which I knew would be coming soon, whether we were ready or not. I thought it would be less stressful to avoid thinking about it. I just assumed that when the time came, it would all work out.

After much discussion, I agreed to try the budget for a few months. Cameron suggested we sit down at the beginning of each month together and talk about where to allocate our income, keeping in mind what "special" expenses we knew we would have that month, like our dog Charlie's yearly physical or our property tax being due. Cameron said this would also be a good time to plan for that extra shopping trip I wanted or the round of golf he was going to play with his friends. The final budget looked nothing like I had expected. There was a budget for buying new books and a budget for saving—the best of both worlds! Maybe this budget thing wasn't so bad after all.

While I was enjoying the budget initially, I also found parts of it uncomfortable because they highlighted some of our spending weaknesses. Cameron and I are both known to push snooze a few too many times in the mornings, which often led to us not having time to make our lunch before work. We found that eating out for lunch one time a week quickly added up to fifty dollars or more a month. That was the perfect amount to try that new restaurant in town we had been wanting to visit, but we didn't have "enough" in the budget to do so.

I also quickly realized that shopping at Target for our groceries each week quickly added up to significantly more than I wanted to spend—mostly because I hated to admit that I couldn't go inside without buying "just" a new shirt or "just" a new rug. I had to admit to myself that even if it didn't feel like I was spending a lot of money, it would quickly add up in the grand scheme of our life. I also learned that you will not save money without trying! Saving money requires planning and effort.

I finally realized that our budget was worthwhile when I needed a new car. My car was old, and we knew the day was fast ap-
proaching when it would be time to get a new one. We saved
each month for the down payment and added the car payment to the budget in preparation. When the time came to
buy the car and have the car payment, it was absolutely no
stress. We knew what we could afford and had proven to ourselves that it fit in the budget. It might have been the least
stressful purchase I had ever made, even though it was the
second most expensive, right after our house! The ease of the
situation proved to us that we were doing the right thing by
budgeting, and I finally agreed with Cameron that it was a
good idea after all.

The benefits of the budget now outweigh any worries I might
have had about it. Though I have to think before spending
money, it has allowed me greater freedom overall. I don't feel
guilty when buying a new dress or going out for that nice dinner because I know before I do it whether it fits in the budget or
not. Budgeting has also improved our communication. We talk
prior to each month and create the budget together, and then,
throughout the month, we communicate to make sure we are
sticking to it. We love having a goal to work towards together!

Through budgeting and conscious saving, we have been able
to do many things that we otherwise wouldn't have been able
to do. We can give to organizations that are important to us,

like our church, send our dog to overnight obedience camp, and even go on vacation to a couple of places on our bucket list. Budgeting requires planning and forethought, but it's an investment worth making!

—Abby

While I think we should all be on a budget—no matter what stage of our lives we are in—I do see times where monthly budgeting may not be necessary after a certain point. This would be appropriate for individuals who have previously proven that they have succeeded in spending and saving for what is truly important to them. This mindset is ingrained in them and they continuously practice this.

Here Are Four Tips for a Successful Budget:

1. Save First.
As mentioned before, if saving and gifting are at the bottom of your budget, utilizing only *whatever is left* at the end of the month, then your budget is upside down.

For folks who tend to cringe at the thought of budgeting but need to save on a consistent basis, I have found a mindset that seems to work for them. To the extent that you can, automate your savings to be the first thing to come out of your paycheck.

Whether that be with your pre-tax deferral to your 401(k) through your employer or a monthly deposit into your Roth IRA, just make it automated and the first thing you do with your income. Then you know that whatever income you have left can be spent freely as a general spending expense. This way, you aren't bogged down by the details of budgeting each month but know you are likely on track, given that you have already hit your savings target.

If charitable gifting is a priority for you, or you would like to make it a priority, then doing something similar to the "savings first" strategy is also beneficial. You may have gotten into the habit of giving whatever is left at the end of the month to charity or scrambling to make some gifts toward the end of the year. If charitable gifting is a priority to you, then this approach will almost never yield the giving level that you would like to reach. Instead, make the charitable gift the first thing you do at the beginning of every month or whenever you receive your paycheck. Giving your first fruits this way will enable you to meet any gifting target you have set for yourself as you periodically give throughout the year.

2. Update Monthly

Update the budget each month to incorporate one-off events such as a dentist appointment you have that month or your sister's birthday that you need to get a present for.

3. Track Carefully

Have a process in place that allows you to track and update your spending throughout the month. There are many online account aggregator tools that will sync to your bank account and allow you to see how you are doing compared to targets. My wife and I just use a shared spreadsheet. It takes a little more manual effort, but that also helps us "feel" our spending more. Whichever method you choose, the overall goal is to have a way for you and your spouse to jointly see where you are for the month/quarter/year and adjust accordingly.

4. Scheduled Check-in

Determine if having a monthly budget is truly necessary for you or if "checking in" on a quarterly or annual basis would be a better fit. A lot of my clients don't need to dig into the details of what they are spending monthly. Others do. The ones who don't, however, can check periodically to see how they are doing compared to their overall target for the year. So, if halfway through the year they see that they are on pace to exceed their annual spending target, then they will know that they need to slow down spending for the remainder of the year. On the other hand, sometimes they are on pace to be under their target for the year, so they then know there is some wiggle room.

Having a set budget for my family has truly enabled us to spend more on things or experiences that mean the most to us. To me, that's what budgeting is all about. Therefore, I'll typically bring my lunch from home most days of the week unless I have a lunch meeting with a friend or some other special occasion. I've gotten out of the habit of going out to lunch just for the heck of it. The ten dollars spent on some restaurant that claims it's not fast food sure does taste good as a temporary feeling, but it doesn't last. I've learned that bringing my lunch has helped save money, which has enabled us to go out to dinner or cook a nice meal on the grill on the weekends. I would rather forgo that temporary feeling during the week at lunch in order to have an experience like going out on the weekend with my wife or a group of friends.

Now, I'm not saying that you have to cut out going out to eat—this isn't that kind of book. I just want to share an example of how budgeting has enabled me to spend more on what I really enjoy. If it's not going out to eat for lunch during the workweek for you, I'm sure there is some expense that could be adjusted so that you have more for something else you value. The following is a personal example of how prioritizing events with family can create lasting memories (versus short-term pleasure only).

For over ten years now, my family has had season tickets for NC State football games. About seven Saturdays a year, we all converge on Raleigh, North Carolina to spend the day together tailgating and cheering on the Pack! Now, these tickets aren't cheap. Plus, you also have to add in the cost of the gas to get to Raleigh, the food for tailgating, and the overall time that we are spending on these Saturdays. The whole process really eats away at our budget, just like I eat away at my Aunt Judy's barbecue ribs and my mom's blonde brownies!

So why do we do this? I mean, the team's record hasn't always been stellar, so our actual return on investment wouldn't be advised by a Certified Financial Planner. Even so, the reason we do this is that we enjoy spending time with family. Despite the high cost and low return on investment, we put in the effort to budget around such events because time with family is important to us.

The point of this story is that when creating your budget, you must consider what priorities you have for your post-savings dollars. Make sure that the amount you budget on certain categories matches what is most important to you. This way, you spend less hard-earned money on short-term pleasures and more on the important things that leave a long-lasting memory.

CHAPTER 2

FAMILY & INVESTING

The riskiest investment you can make is leaving your investment in cash.[3]

What?!

It sure feels safe to leave your money in cash at the bank or in your 401(k). From the cash-holder's perspective, when they see the worry and anxiety-driven news that comes across the television or social media news feed about the big losses in the stock market, they sit back and smile. Their portfolio balance doesn't decline, given the cash investment.

Yes, you should have a portion of your portfolio in cash or other conservative investments, but having too much in cash truly is risky! Let me explain.

The expected rate of return you can anticipate from your cash holding is minimal, especially in comparison to a long-term stock or bond investment. Often, cash won't even keep pace with inflation, causing your dollar deposited today to have less purchasing power when you spend it years from now. With your expenses rising at the cost of inflation (cost of living adjustment or COLA), if your investments aren't keeping up with this, then you will find yourself needing to decrease your standard of living in the future, as your savings won't be enough to cover your spending. The opportunity cost of not investing in more than cash can be tremendous, as I will show you in a later example.

My grandfather (Pops) used to take us out on the canoe on a local lake in southern New Hampshire. We would often go up for a week while we were out of school to visit him and my grandmother (JoJo). My parents, my sister, and I would pack up Pop's Chevy Blazer with supplies, along with and the dogs (Luke and Penny). Then we'd strap the canoe to the top and head off to the lake.

What I really remember from these trips occurred each year during the car ride. We would stop for gas or for a bite to eat, and Pops would reach into the center console and pull out an old burlap bag. Stitched in the side of the bag were the words "Bertie County Peanuts." Now, this referred to Bertie County, North Carolina, as they are known for their peanuts, but there were no peanuts in this bag. There was cash—and lots of it! I never knew why he had so much cash in this burlap sack, but it was always there, summer after summer. I imagine it had always been there, many years prior to our first canoe trip.

Since then, I've wondered, what if he had put that money in an IRA or another investment account for ten-plus years instead of letting it sit in the center console of that Chevy Blazer? Invested appropriately, could it have doubled in size? Was he too nervous to put that money in the stock market in the first place? Who knows? But it is kind of like the "stuffing money in your mattress" way of saving. While it is comforting to know that it is always there, was it really the best decision for long-term saving and investing?

There is a parable in the Bible about three servants and their investment decisions with their master's money that I want to share with you. It comes from Matthew 25:14–30, New Living Translation (NLT).

The Parable of the Three Servants[4]

"Again, the Kingdom of Heaven can be illustrated by the story of a man going on a long trip. He called together his servants and entrusted his money to them while he was gone. He gave five bags of silver to one, two bags of silver to another, and one bag of silver to the last—dividing it in proportion to their abilities. He then left on his trip.

"The servant who received the five bags of silver began to invest the money and earned five more. The servant with two bags of silver also went to work and earned two more. But the servant who received the one bag of silver dug a hole in the ground and hid the master's money.

"After a long time their master returned from his trip and called them to give an account of how they had used his money. The servant to whom he had entrusted the five bags of silver came forward with five more and said, "Master, you gave me five bags of silver to invest, and I have earned five more.""

"The master was full of praise. 'Well done, my good and faithful servant. You have been faithful in handling this small amount, so now I will give you many more re- sponsibilities. Let's celebrate together!'

"The servant who had received the two bags of silver came forward and said, 'Master, you gave me two bags of silver to invest, and I have earned two more.'

"The master said, 'Well done, my good and faithful servant. You have been faithful in handling this small amount, so now I will give you many more responsibili- ties. Let's celebrate together!'

"Then the servant with the one bag of silver came and said, 'Master, I knew you were a harsh man, harvesting crops you didn't plant and gathering crops you didn't cultivate. I was afraid I would lose your money, so I hid it in the earth. Look, here is your money back.'

"But the master replied, 'You wicked and lazy servant! If you knew I harvested crops I didn't plant and gathered crops I didn't cultivate, why didn't you deposit my money in the bank? At least I could have gotten some interest on it.'

"Then he ordered, 'Take the money from this servant, and give it to the one with the ten bags of silver. To those who use well what they are given, even more will be given, and they will have an abundance. But from those who do nothing, even what little they have will be taken away. Now throw this useless servant into outer darkness, where there will be weeping and gnashing of teeth.'"

So, in my story, it appears that Pops chose the route of digging a hole and hiding his money in the earth. While the money was never lost in the center console of that old Chevy Blazer, he also may have missed out on an opportunity to invest that money and watch it grow over a long period of time. However, the anxiety about investing often is the reason we delay or never invest our money to begin with. Think for a minute, though: Have you ever looked back and thought "That was really productive to worry about that decision. I'm so glad that I lost sleep over investing in the stock market." Likely not.

Have the Right Mindset

It is important, however, to have the right mindset when investing. To make my point, I must digress a bit.

My wife and I have always tried to plan all the dinners for the week so that we aren't scrambling last minute to make dinner and then just decide to get take-out. This practice has financial and health benefits. However, even when planning dinners for the week, we aren't always in the mood to cook and prepare our dinner after a long day of work, especially as the week goes on. By about Wednesday or Thursday, we find ourselves straying away from our planned dinners and are tempted to run to Tijuana Flats for a starter of chips and queso and our dos tacos and beef and black bean burrito entrees.

We recently found that the solution to our desire to waver from our plan later in the week is to utilize the slow cooker that had been sitting on our shelf since we received it as a wedding present. We use a tag-team approach. My wife prepares the food (usually fajita-seasoned chicken) before she leaves for work in the morning. Then, before I leave for work, I take the prepared dinner, plug the slow cooker into the wall, and stir the contents. As you can see, I got the better part of that deal!

When we come home from work, our dinner has been slow cooking all day and is ready for us to eat! Even if we are tired and out of energy by the end of the workweek, it doesn't take much time or effort to serve ourselves the dinner that has been cooking all day.

So why do I bring up our weekly dinner habits? The idea behind the slow cooker—putting in work in the morning to enjoy an easy meal at the end of the day—is a good metaphor for long-term investments.

For the majority of you reading this book, retirement savings are considered a long-term investment, one in which you consistently put aside money in your company's 401(k) plan or your own investment account, but don't plan on using any of the savings until your retirement. When you first began, the growth in your account was likely very slow. You may have been in your early career and weren't able to save as much money each pay period as you are now. Over time, though, you started increasing your contributions and began to see the effects of compound interest, hopefully paving the way for a retirement nest egg that can support your lifestyle throughout your retirement years.

Do you see the similarities between investing for the long term and cooking in a crock pot? Each item requires some up-front preparation followed by routine maintenance and a length of time to develop, but at the end of the day, you can enjoy the finished product.

CAMERON HENDRICKS

Did you catch that term "compound interest" that I slipped into the slow cooker example? If you have been investing for a while, you will likely have seen the effects of compound interest in your personal accounts, but if not, let me walk you through an example.

Imagine you were given these two options: receive $1 million today or receive one penny doubled every day for the next month? The $1 million deal sounds pretty good, especially when we are comparing it to pennies. But let's look at the math of what a penny can do when doubled every day for a month.[5]

Day 1: $.01
Day 2: $.02
Day 3: $.04
Day 4: $.08
Day 5: $.16
Day 6: $.32
Day 7: $.64
Day 8: $1.28
Day 9: $2.56
Day 10: $5.12
Day 11: $10.24
Day 12: $20.48
Day 13: $40.96
Day 14: $81.92

Day 15: $163.84
Day 16: $327.68
Day 17: $655.36
Day 18: $1,310.72
Day 19: $2,621.44
Day 20: $5,242.88
Day 21: $10,485.76
Day 22: $20,971.52
Day 23: $41,943.04
Day 24: $83,886.08
Day 25: $167,772.16
Day 26: $335,544.32
Day 27: $671,088.64
Day 28: $1,342,177.28
Day 29: $2,684,354.56
Day 30: $5,368,709.12

It's hard to believe that one penny, doubled every day for a month, gives you over $5 million! While this is a bit of an extreme example, as our money likely isn't doubling every day, this does show the power of compound interest. It reverts back to the tremendous opportunity cost of investing your assets in nothing more than cash.

In the early stages of compound interest, nothing too exciting happens. You can see that in the example above. For most of the month, from a total dollar amount standpoint, you would have been better off taking the $1 million up-front—until you get to day 28 of the month, in which the benefits of choosing the penny really show up. Not shown here is day 31, in which the amount doubled from day 30 would be over $10 million!

Once again, you shouldn't expect your money to double each day, but this example does show the power of the slow, almost boring, early stages of saving until the compound interest really kicks in, producing larger dollar amounts. It would have been nice to know the wonders of compound interest when I was a child and picking up weeds at my grandpa's house at a nickel per weed. Maybe I should have counteroffered my wage to be a penny doubled every day!

The psychological and emotional aspect of an investor's behavior often affects the investment decisions they make. This can be especially so around times of life-changing events such as additions to the family, retirement, or other large changes to your financial situation. Other common times for this to occur are after a long-tenured underperformance or outperformance of the market. I've seen all of the above events associated with some of the following behavioral investing effects that may cause you to be a "no-investing somebody!"

Overconfidence

The most common result of strong portfolio performance is overconfidence in your investing ability. Often, strong performance comes from short-term stock picking, in which, over that short period of time, outperformance was achieved based on a "hunch" or a tip about a stock heard on the radio that sounded good. While this stock picking may work in the short term, it often leads to long-term underperformance. The individual has success with a few stocks, so they try their hand at picking more, and this is where they get into the trouble of over-trading and trying to time the market.

I remember, as a child, playing basketball daily in our driveway, practicing my shot to be the next star college basketball player in the tradition-rich Tobacco Road part of the Atlantic Coast Conference. Shooting alone one morning, I made shot after shot and decided that I must be pretty good at this basketball thing. So, when my dad came out of the house, I made a wager with him that if I made my next shot, he owed me a quarter. He laughed and agreed, likely knowing that he was getting ready to teach me a lesson I wouldn't forget. To my disbelief, I missed that shot with a whole quarter riding on it, which was a big deal to a kid that was too young to work for money. My overconfidence led me to believe that I was better than I actually was, and while my short-term performance was great, I quickly lost it all with one miss.

The short-term investing game is not for the individual who wants to provide a strong financial resource for their family and the generations to come. A disciplined investment strategy with decisions based on long-term goals and objectives is what will lead to *true overconfidence.*

Familiarity Bias

Another investing shortfall that many individuals run into is
the concept of familiarity bias. This could be investing solely or
heavily in the country that you live in or having a large portion
of your portfolio in your own company's stock. These are the
most common examples that I have come across when discussing portfolio allocation with clients and prospective clients.

I do want to touch on the example regarding the company
stock for a minute. When you have a bias towards your company, not only can your 401(k) largely be allocated to the company stock, but your income is also reliant on the company as
well. So not only would your retirement savings suffer if the
company had troubles, but your job itself and the income you
receive from it could be in jeopardy. Now, this could, of course,
swing the other way if the company were to be very successful,
but what you should be looking for in your financial situation is
good diversification, whether that be your retirement accounts
or even your income. A good rule of thumb for company stock
in your portfolio is no more than 10 percent.

In regard to familiarity bias and the country you live in, almost
80 percent of US equities are held by investors who live in the
United States, according to a recent study by Vanguard.[6] This
isn't too surprising, though, given that the United States makes
up about 50 percent of the global index weighting. However,
some of the other countries in the study had even more home

country familiarity bias, especially given their low global index weighting. For example, Canada equities only have a 3.4 percent global index weighting, but Canadian investors hold almost 60 percent of them. The point here is that familiarity bias can apply not only to the type of investment but also the country where that investment is held.

Hindsight Bias

Hindsight bias refers to when an investor believes they predicted a particular past event when, in fact, they did not. This leads to overconfidence and the investor thinking they can predict future events.

This can also apply to looking at past returns of the investment choices in your 401(k). It's easy to look at the fund choices in your 401(k) and choose to invest in the funds with the highest recent performance. This could, however, prove to be the opposite of what you should do. Let me explain through the example shown in the table[7] below:

	Returns previous 10 Years, 4/30/96–4/30/06	Returns Last 10 10 Years, 4/30/06–4/30/16
Russell 1000 Lg. Cap Growth	6.2%	8.2%
Russell 1000 Lg. Cap Value	11.2%	5.7%

Imagine you are back in the mid-2000s, and you see that your *Large Cap Value* holdings outperformed your *Large Cap Growth* holdings. So, when choosing how to invest your future account contributions, you would choose the *Large Cap Value fund*, right?

Well, if you had done so, you would have underperformed the Growth funds over the next ten years! Fund performance can often go in cycles depending on if certain fund areas (growth/value or sectors like energy/financials/technology, etc.) are out of favor.

Naive Diversification

While you have heard me previously mention diversification when discussing the familiarity bias, there is such a thing as naive diversification. We've all heard the phrase "don't put all your eggs in one basket." Well, I would like to add a new phrase to go along with that: "Don't put all of your eggs into every single basket you see."

Consider your 401(k) for a minute. If you have a 401(k), likely has twenty to thirty different fund choices that you can choose to invest in. Now, think about how many you hold specifically. Is it four or five, or is it ten to fifteen? If the answer is closer to ten to fifteen, then you are likely experiencing naive diversification firsthand.

With so many fund options, you may think it's wise to put a little bit of your account balance in all of them. What if your particular 401(k) has five US large-cap choices and one international holding, among which you split your balance? In doing so, you think you are diversified with so many holdings, but in reality, you may not be and are just practicing naive diversification.

With all of these behavioral investing examples, the most important thing to do is to look at your own portfolio, especially at times in your life when big events are taking place or at times when the market has made big swings up or down, and see what you have done in the past in these situations. Take a step back and look at your portfolio through the lens of someone else, who may not be emotionally attached to the outcome of your investments. Did you correctly respond to the last bear market? What about in the years leading up to your children going off to college? Did you try to squeeze in some last-minute returns in their 529 account when they were seniors in high school and you thought the market was going to go up? Did you get burned in this situation and have a couple thousand fewer dollars to cover tuition payments? While this scenario may be dramatic, it makes you think about the decisions you have made with your investments, especially in situations where you were just trying to help your family.

These previously mentioned behavioral concepts that persist in our investing decisions often result in lower returns in our portfolios. Typically, at extreme points in the market, fund flows into the market will vary depending on the emotions of the investor. A couple of industry leaders conducted studies on this, noting the average investor behavioral impact to their portfolios. The following are their conclusions.

Morningstar did a study titled "Mind the Gap 2014."[8] They found that in 2009, during the financial crisis that began in 2008, money was flowing out of stock funds. However, this time period in 2009 ended up being the bottom of the market, and therefore one of the *worst* times to pull money out of stock positions. As a result of behavioral trends, investors underperformed in the fund returns that they were invested in. Over the ten-year period ending 12/31/2013 investors underperformed the fund return by an average of 2.49 percent. In other words, the investor only gained 4.8 percent over those ten years while the typical fund they were invested in gained 7.3 percent. This could result from the previously mentioned fund flows, among other factors. The specific returns for different asset classes varied as well, with international funds and sector funds showing the widest discrepancy with over 3 percent return difference. This ties in with our discussion on past returns determining your choices in your 401(k); the past returns don't necessarily mean that the *investors* who held those funds actually got the returns that the funds earned.

Vanguard also highlights the behavioral aspect of the average investor in a recent study, "The Added Value of Financial

Advisors."[9] From their research, they state, "Recent Vanguard research shows that your advisor not only adds peace of mind, but also may add about 3 percentage points of value in net portfolio returns over time. What does this mean? Your advisor has the ability and the time to evaluate your portfolio investments, meet with you to discuss objectives, and help get you through tough markets. All of these factored together potentially add value to your net returns (returns after taxes and fees) over time."

The research study then breaks down the areas of how a financial advisor can potentially add about 3 percent to your returns over time. Any guesses on what component of a financial advisor's job may provide the biggest return? Most investors would guess that stock picking or choosing the best fund to outperform the market would be the biggest benefit of having a financial advisor, and they would be incorrect. The study found that "Behavioral Coaching" could add about 1.5 percent to your net return over time. So about half of the value that advisors provide, according to the study, comes from behavioral coaching. Specifically, this means the overall guidance the advisor provides to help the investor adhere to their financial plan. This is particularly applicable during tough market conditions or big life changes that could potentially influence financial decisions negatively.

I frequently get asked this question by my clients: "Compared to someone else my age, how am I doing?" It seems to be human nature to want to compare our performance to a benchmark or to those around us.

When it comes to investments, it is common to compare our performance against indices such as the S&P 500 or MSCI EAFE. In the United States, though, the S&P 500 seems to be the one that comes up most frequently when I hear investors comparing their performance to a benchmark. This was the case in a recent meeting with a client, in which he pointed out that while he can regularly see his portfolio balance and returns, he didn't know what he should be benchmarking to see if he was on the right track. His first instinct was to compare returns to the S&P 500 (A US-based stock index), which I explained wasn't the best place to compare, given that his portfolio was diversified and couldn't be compared to just one index. On top of that, I made the comment that you shouldn't assess your whole financial situation based solely on the returns of your portfolio compared to indices or the returns of individuals such as coworkers or family members.

Each of us has our own unique situation comprised of our personal goals and objectives. We have invested and planned our finances around what is important to us. For example, you may be saving for your children's college education, and it is one of your top priorities to pay for 100 percent of their education. Given the expense of college, your financial portfolio will likely look much different from your neighbor who doesn't plan on paying for their children's college expenses. So, even if you and your neighbor are similar ages and have similar incomes, your investment portfolios will look different because of your personal goals and objectives.

So, what should you be comparing your account balance and performance to? You should have a comprehensive financial plan in place that has been built to include things that are most important to you. It will include your cash flow based on your income and expenses. Your expenses will include the desired college expenses for your children, annual charitable gifting, and family vacations, as well as all other aspects of your financial life. This plan will be tailored specifically to you and will provide you with the road map to your ideal financial life. THIS is what you want to compare your account balances and investment returns to. Only the financial plan that portrays your situation will provide you with a true benchmark of whether or not you are on track.

In saying that, our financial lives are always changing and therefore impacting our financial plans. This is what we call the irreducible uncertainty. Our life events and market conditions are going to constantly alter our financial plan. This is okay, though, as we can always update the plan, but it's how we respond to these altering events that really impacts our financial situation.

CHAPTER 3

FAMILY & RETIREMENT PLANNING

L ook at just about any website for a financial advisor or investment custodian, and you will likely see pictures of sailboats, a lighthouse, or a couple playing golf together. After all, this is what we see when we picture our retirement years, right? You worked for this your whole life, and now you want to have a relaxing retirement enjoying the money you have saved as your nest egg.

While this may be the stereotypical view of retirement, it might not be the ideal retirement picture for you! The first thing you need to do when considering retirement is to decide what you want your retirement to look like. It basically comes down to two questions: "What do you want to spend your time doing and what do you want to spend your resources on?"

In order to answer these questions, you have to take a step back and actually do some planning for your retirement. It's funny.

I once heard that the average person spends more time preparing for a two-week vacation than they do for a forty-year retirement.[10] Consider the following three thought-provoking questions for the pre-retiree when making the effort to plan for the retirement that you imagine.

1. Why do you want to retire, and what do you want your retirement to look like?

After working for forty years, why do you want to retire now? Is this the way you always envisioned it, and you just up and quit one day in your mid-sixties? Do you dream about playing golf all day and sipping mojitos on a beach somewhere? If so, then great! Just make sure you know why you want to retire and how you want to live your retirement. If your dream is the stereotypical retirement that we see on television commercials, then go for it!

However, maybe you can't see yourself taking life that slowly and might even be bored in a stereotypical retirement. In this case, maybe going from full-time to part-time employment is a better fit for you so you can gradually retire. Or maybe you want to "retire" from your current career and then begin a second career. This could be doing something that has always interested you—maybe you have been doing it as a hobby but now want to take it to the next level. In fact, most entrepreneurs aren't young "twenty-somethings" in Silicon Valley playing on their smartphones. Most entrepreneurs are actually in their fifties![11]

2. You have been saving all this money for all these years, but what is this money *for*, anyway?

You spent year after year saving diligently every pay period in your company's 401(k). You took advantage of the employer match and even spent many hours attempting to figure out what fund you should invest in. Have you ever stopped for a minute and thought about what all these savings were really for? If you're like most people, it's to have resources to use when you retire, because when you retire, you'll have little to no income. Right? Well, yes, that is true. But what do your savings mean to you?

Your savings are there to enrich your life and provide peace of mind. They are there to enjoy with your family. Maybe your savings are there so that you can be generous to those in need. Maybe your savings are there to help you switch careers to something that you have always wanted to do—something you'll never want to retire from because you love your job so much.

3. When will your retirement start, and how long will it last?

The truth is, we can plan for this question all we want, but we may not have much control over the "when" or the "how long." In fact, 20 to 25 percent of retirements are forced to begin earlier than planned.[12] This may be due to company layoffs, health reasons, or other issues that may be beyond our control.

So what do you do in these situations? You need to once again find something that motivates you, especially if you need more resources than previously anticipated to sustain your retirement. What meaningful work or activity can you find that will fuel you to have a fulfilled second career or retirement?

On the other hand, how long do you need to plan for your retirement to last? Once again, we may not have a whole lot of say in this. It depends a lot on our health status, and we just can't know when "our time" will come.

You have to determine how you want to live the rest of your life. This goes beyond retirement. Ask yourself: How do you view your life? While that may be a deeper question than you were expecting to be asked while reading this chapter, I think it merits attention.

A Retirement Mindset

On average, the more educated you are, the longer you live. While this statement may be quite general in nature, it is actually a proven fact.[13]

You may have graduated from college thirty years ago, or you may have never gone to college at all. You may potentially believe that your education days are behind you, but how do you keep up your skills? How do you continue to develop intellectually? After all, the statistics don't lie—the more you learn, the greater chance you have for a longer life.

A few resources that I am currently using include podcasts, webinars, online courses, and, of course, reading books. It has been my experience that these resources not only increase my knowledge and intellectual mindset but also help me to have a more positive outlook on life. I have seen this in many aspects of my life, but one that I think may be particularly impactful is the positive viewpoint on aging.

For years, I have heard many women claim to celebrate their twenty-ninth birthday for the fourth year in a row (or the fortieth), but is that really the mindset we want to have? In reality, I've read that people who have a positive viewpoint on aging live seven to eight years longer![14] It seems difficult, however, to have a positive viewpoint on aging if you don't have a positive outlook on your life.

Another trait of those who live longer is, not surprisingly, that they are healthier. While this is not a health book, this fact does relate to your retirement, and I'll explain. Studies show that every additional year you work increases your lifespan by eleven percent. Challenging your body and mind for one extra year can increase your lifespan. Therefore, the number-one reason people leave retirement and return to work isn't because of boredom or financial reasons; it's actually to maintain their health.[15]

This all circles back to having a plan and knowing what we want our lives to look like, and, in this case, what we want our retirement to look like. Typically, we associate retirement planning as strictly a financial matter, but as you can see from the last few paragraphs, the financial aspect is only one component in the larger picture.

Study Others' Retirements

Think of all the people you know who have retired, and consider who has retired "well" and who hasn't. Did they seem to flawlessly transition into retirement and continue to thrive? Or did they stumble out of the gate and have a hard time gaining their footing in their retirement years? Studying the retirement experiences of others can help you see how you want yours to look, whether you have yet to retire or are already in retirement.

A study done by Merrill Lynch called the "Age Wave"[16] shows data on the preferred way to retire. It surprised me to learn that only 28 percent of people claimed they never wanted to engage in paid work another day in their lives. Judging by the number of white sand beaches and pristine golf course depictions of retirement we see on television, I thought for sure this number would at least be over half!

If only 28 percent said they never wanted to work for pay again, what did the others envision their preferred retirement to look like? Well, 35 percent said they wanted to work part-time, and 33 percent said they would like to cycle between work and leisure. In all, that means about 68 percent said they planned to continue working in some capacity that was not full-time in nature.

So why even retire in the first place? If most of us don't want to stop working, then why do we do it? If the concept of retirement didn't exist, would you stop working just because you reached a specific age? Maybe you enjoy what you are doing, and your health and career choice allows you to continue. If that is the case, then why retire just because you are now sixty-two, sixty-five, sixty-seven, etc.?

Retirement shouldn't be defined by an age or even a financial number. It should be defined by your state of mind and the feasibility of financial freedom. On the other hand, maybe you are one of those people who is counting down the days until you can completely retire. You've spent years begrudgingly braving the commuter traffic to sit in an office all day, surrounded by people you don't necessarily care for, doing work you don't like, and you just need a change. In order to determine what kind of retirement is best for you, consider the true reason *why* you are ready to "hang it up." The following are just a few of the most common reasons.[17]

1. You are burnt out. Maybe the example I just mentioned— with the commuter traffic and the work you don't like—hits home for you. You just feel like you are tired and "over it." You've had to deal with the corporate structure for years, and you can't take it anymore. Or you started your own business years ago, but the direction your business has now gone wasn't as you originally intended and has taken a toll on you.

2. You are disinterested. You have gotten to the point where your job no longer interests you enough to make you want to continue doing it for much longer. I often compare these individuals to the entrepreneur who starts a business. They thrive in the building stage and enjoy overseeing the growth and success of their business, but over time, the thrill and adrenaline they received from the initial startup is no longer there. They have essentially "been there and done that." Often, they would rather be starting a *new* business that would align more closely with their interests and passions.

3. You are bored. Our careers often provide challenges for us—new clients, new technology, or new processes or systems that we develop. What happens, however, when the challenges go away? You don't feel as useful as you once did, and you don't feel you are making as big a difference as you would like in your company or in the lives of others.

If any of these three reasons stand out to you as reasons that you want to retire, then maybe you are not quite ready for full-blown retirement. Instead, you may be better suited for a kind of retirement where you just take a step back for a while. This could be an extended vacation for a few months or even a few years. It could be a time to reassess your priorities or a time to recharge the batteries and catch up on some of the things you have been putting off that you always wanted to do. Maybe take that trip to a far corner of the United States or around the world. Try out that hobby you piddle around with on the weekends—the one you've always wanted to make a more concerted effort toward to turn it into something special. Maybe it's woodworking or monogramming. Whatever it is, give it a shot!

This break should not be confused with full-blown retirement. There is a reason it is called a "break" period. At some point, you are going to get that itch to get back out there and work. This would be consistent with the desires of 68 percent of people from the previously mentioned study who either want to work part-time or cycle between work and leisure.

So before planning on retiring abruptly to play golf every day or just visit with your grandchildren, first consider if that is really what you see yourself doing long-term. Will that lifestyle keep you energized and wanting to get out of bed each day? Will you continue to grow intellectually and maintain a level of health to keep you going? If the answers to these questions are "yes," then this type of retirement may be right for you. However, if you answer "no" to these questions, then make it a point to seek out work or volunteer opportunities during your break in order to keep your skills up so that you can re-enter the workforce in some capacity when you are ready.

Retiring Well in Primetime TV

I want to share a story of someone who was floundering in retirement. It actually comes from a person I've never met or even talked to. Even so, I feel like I know him pretty well, given that my wife and I binge-watched him via Netflix on the hit show *Parks and Recreation*.

In the last episode of the final season, the character Ron Swanson retires from his construction company job, which was actually a second career following his long stint as head of the titular Parks and Recreation Department. In this episode, Ron hints at some of the common reasons people want to retire. In this case, he felt that he had completed all there was to do, and he was no longer needed at the construction company. Upon retirement, Ron is shown in a sorry state, as he no longer feels useful. He no longer has a purpose for getting out of bed in the morning.

Knowing that he needs a change, Ron reaches out to his old work acquaintance Leslie, who is always willing to help others, and she begins searching for a job in which Ron would feel useful during his retirement. Leslie pulls some strings and is able to land him a job as the new superintendent of a National

Park. Being the avid outdoorsman that he is, Ron is immediately overjoyed.

The point of this story is to show an example of the reality of retirement for many people. This fictional character, Ron Swanson, represents what early retirees often find in real life: permanent vacation isn't necessarily a "vacation." The fact that *Parks and Recreation* addressed this issue reveals that this occurrence is more mainstream than you might think. Maybe vacations during our working years are only as fun as they are because they are a *break* from work. If your permanent vacation becomes too much like work, and you feel obligated to endure it, then it clearly doesn't live up to the retirement you imagined.

Are You Financially Prepared for Retirement?

So far, we have focused primarily on what you want your retirement to look like and what factors play a role in choosing to fully retire or continue working in some capacity. While these scenarios are played out in our preferred visions of retirement, the reality that we may not be able to fulfill these retirement desires is certainly a possibility for many. How do we prepare financially, so that we can live out our preferred retirement scenarios?

Many people work continuously for about forty years, always having the income to buy groceries, pay the electricity bill, go to the movies, or choose other entertainment options. Even doing so, many are able to save a little for retirement and some for other large expenses such as their children's college educations or weddings. But how are all these expenses covered during retirement?

Historically, this retirement income came from three main areas: personal savings such as a 401(k) or IRA, a pension, and Social Security. Pensions have been decreasing in popularity for years, and with potential future changes to Social Security, the need for personal savings has increased dramatically—especially when considering the potential for an abrupt end to constant, salaried income while expenses stay the same or even potentially increase. All this is added to the desire for trips or activities planned immediately upon retirement.

To get a better view of the typical spending pattern for retirees, visualize the smile you would draw on a stick figure, or, for those more technologically advanced, picture the smiley face emoji. The inverted bell curve shape of a smile portrays the spending patterns of many retirees. Early in their retirement, when they have the energy and desire to travel and take up new activities, they spend more. Then, as they age, their energy levels may decrease, and therefore, spending falls as they are less active. Finally, toward the end of life, the smile peaks back up to the opposite corner of the mouth, and spending tends to increase, normally as a result of medical and health-related expenses.

So the question then becomes, "How do we know if we have saved enough?" The answer on the surface is pretty simple, actually, in that you just need a plan! Of course, this plan can be complicated, especially when we don't always know what surprises are around the corner.

Having a plan helps you set your priorities and financially prepare for them. One example that typically comes up for those with younger children is the priority to help their children pay for college and, in some cases, cover *all* their college expenses. This is a tough one, given the high cost of college and expected increases in college costs, which we will discuss later in the Family & College Planning chapter. Given this, we are often faced with the choice between saving for retirement or helping our children pay for college. I like the way that the nationally known authority on paying for college, Troy Onink, puts it: "College is a toll booth on the road to retirement."[18]

His point is that college planning and retirement planning are not mutually exclusive. These two items are major components of our financial lives that just so happen to coincide with each other. While overwhelming at times, the complexity also creates opportunities to more efficiently plan for both. We will cover some of these strategies in a later chapter, where I discuss how to best plan financially for your children and grandchildren's college educations.

Desires in Retirement

Another common priority that comes up close to retirement is the desire to buy a second home. Often, this desire arises when children are reaching their late teens and college years, and the parents want to create a neutral place for them to spend time with their family—something different than their hometown home, but a place that can be like a second home to them as well.

At first glance, these second homes don't seem all that expensive. They may be half the price of your primary residence. However, maintaining a beach, lake, or mountain home on top of keeping up your personal residence can become a significant expense. For those who may not be financially ready to take on a second home, one option can be downsizing your primary home, especially if your children are grown. Using the equity from the home you sold, you can purchase a smaller primary residence and potentially have funds to put toward a second home. The smaller house decreases the maintenance, property tax, and general overall upkeep of having two homes.

Nick Saban's Story

College football has always been a major interest of mine. Recently, I've been listening to coaches' speeches to players and the media, in which they often discuss topics outside of football. At NC State, they have a session each week called "Real World Wednesdays," in which they usually bring in an outside speaker to discuss with the team a topic that will help them become better people outside of their time on the football field. Urban Meyer (Ohio State), Dabo Swinney (Clemson) and Nick Saban (Alabama) are three coaches who have really stood out to me as providing insights into life beyond football. So when I recently saw a feature[19] on Nick Saban welcoming ESPN to his lake home, I was intrigued to see what it was all about.

At first, I thought it was going to be like the old *MTV Cribs* episodes where a celebrity takes the camera crew through their home, showing off the eight-car garage or the ten-seat movie theater. However, we never really saw the inside of Coach Saban's lake home. Instead, the camera crew visited with him in the backyard and then went for a ride around the lake on Saban's pontoon boat. So what does all of this have to do with a book about family and finance, you ask? Well, you would think that during the interview with Saban, they primarily discussed football or the upcoming season, but early in the interview, Saban was already talking about his family.

Saban's lake home provided a place for him and his family to spend valuable time together and create memories to last a lifetime. He stated that as he had gotten older, these family moments had become more and more important to him. Early in his career, he'd been constantly grinding and hustling to advance his career and win more games, often leading to times where he had to move his family around the country or miss out on his kids' activities. Now, more advanced in his career and in age, he realized how much time he'd missed with family. He now cherishes the moments they have at the lake home.

Well, Nick Saban's lakefront home sounds nice, especially if you saw the interview with the house in the background: a central place where family can gather to spend time together, no matter where life has taken them around the country or the world. They can always depend on the lake house to revert back to family time in a relaxed environment.

You may be thinking, "He's Nick Saban, though with multiple national championships at Alabama. He is consistently one of the highest-paid coaches in college football; it must be easy for him to buy a lakefront home." You are probably right. The ability to have a lake home comes from the combination of his finances with the value he places on family time. But let's dig into this a little deeper. While Nick Saban's story highlights a lake home, the same could apply to any type of second home, such as a beach house or mountain home.

A number of times, I have heard clients express such goals and aspirations for the next chapter of life, which typically starts when they have children who are in college or have just recently graduated. Now that they have paid for their children to go to college, their financial minds shift focus more towards retirement. They can now ramp their 401(k) contributions back up so that they can build their nest egg as they approach retirement age. This typically works for a year or two, but then the client gets a little bored with the 401(k) savings and begins to think more about what they are really saving for and why they are so focused on retirement. Their mindset begins to shift after becoming empty-nesters.

While each individual has their own desires for this empty-nester lifestyle, it often leads to wanting a second home! Given my office's proximity to the North Carolina beaches, this usually leads to my clients looking into buying a beach home. So I sit down with these clients, and we discuss why they want to buy a beach home and how they will make the purchase. Where will the money come from? As you remember, these individuals are often trying to save up enough money for retirement themselves, so finding extra money for a beach home sounds a little daunting.

As we continue to discuss the situation, it becomes clear that having this second home has become a priority for them. I like when this happens because when people establish what is really important to them, they are usually more willing to cut back in other areas of their life in order to make the purchase in a financially sound way.

This age range of client usually has a decent-sized house that was ideal when the kids were growing up, before they set out for college, but now, the house sits half-empty except when the kids come home for Thanksgiving and Christmas. Given the number of years that they have lived in the house, there is usually a low balance on the mortgage and therefore, pretty high equity in the house. In this case, downsizing starts to make sense. Downsizing your primary residence and then using the sale proceeds to purchase a smaller and less expensive home could also enable you to purchase a second home that could be used as a centralized meeting place for the family.

Really, what this all boils down to isn't retirement for the sake of retiring; nor does it come down to buying second homes (this is just an example I commonly come across). What it comes down to is being financially independent and being able to do the things that you desire financially in order to enjoy time with your family while utilizing the financial resources that you worked so hard to create.

CHAPTER 4

FAMILY & GIFTING

Typically when I see a gift given, whether it is to a family member or charitable organization, the gifted asset is cash. You may be surprised to hear that cash is often the worst asset to gift. Of course, the recipient is fine with it; after all, everyone likes to receive cash! However, have you ever considered that other assets in your portfolio may be more advantageous for you to gift?

Let's imagine you have a mixture of stock and bond mutual funds that you would like to gift to friends, family, and your favorite charity. It's not as simple as just going down the list and picking a random fund from your portfolio to gift. There is some strategy involved that will benefit you and those receiving the gifts.

Some things you should consider include:

1. Consider the appreciation of the holdings in your portfolio.

In a taxable investment account, the basis and sub-sequential gain or loss will be tracked throughout the time you hold that stock. Upon selling that stock, you will owe capital gains on the amount above the original basis (what you bought the stock for). On the other hand, you could have a capital loss if the current market value is actually less than the basis or what you bought it for.

Whenever you have a large, unrealized gain and want to gift that fund, the best place to gift would be a charitable organization. The reason for this is you will not have to pay capital gains on that fund once gifted. This is a win-win situation because the charitable organization that receives the fund actually does not have to pay the gains either.

Whenever you have an unrealized loss in a stock fund that you own, your best option is to keep that fund for yourself. If you still want to gift it, you could sell the fund and therefore be able to utilize the loss on your tax return, and then you could give the sale proceeds as cash.

2. Consider the income needs of the individual receiving the gift.

For example, you may have an income-producing bond mutual fund that you want to gift to a family member. Your young child or grandchild would not be an ideal option for this gift, as they are likely not in a position of needing income.

An individual who could benefit more from that income-producing fund would be an elderly parent or other retired individual. While they likely could use the income, another benefit of them being retired is that they potentially have a low-income tax bracket, and therefore, the additional income from the income-producing fund would not be a big tax burden for them.

While a young child or grandchild may not be the most suitable candidate for an income-producing fund, they would be an ideal candidate to receive the gift of a stock fund with high future expected appreciation. While not producing a lot of income, the fund provides long-term growth, which the child can take advantage of, as they have time on their side and can hold on to the fund over a long period of time.

To illustrate what we have just walked though, I have included the following example to illustrate various assets for gifting and their ideal recipients.

Let's say you have four holdings in your portfolio that you would like to gift. You are considering distributing the assets to some of the following people:

1. Your child
2. Your parent
3. Your favorite charity
4. Yourself

	Fair Market Value	Cost Basis	Yield	Projected Future Appreciation
Lg. Cap Mutual Fund #1	$10,000	$2,000	1%	4%
Lg. Cap Mutual Fund #2	$10,000	$5,000	0%	10%
Bond Mutual Fund #1	$10,000	$10,000	6%	1%
Bond Mutual Fund #2	$10,000	$15,000	3%	0%

1. *Your child:* You should gift the "Large Cap Mutual Fund #2" to your child since it has the greatest future appreciation. Your child likely doesn't need a gift that produces income (yield), but would best be suited for a holding that will produce high returns over a long period of time and be able to take advantage of compound interest.

2. *Your parent:* You should gift "Bond Mutual Fund #1" to your parent because of the high yield percentage this holding produces. Your parents may be retired

and in need of an income-producing holding. If they are retired, they likely will be in a low tax bracket and therefore not owe as much taxes on the income produced.

3. *Your favorite charity:* You should gift "Large Cap Mutual Fund #1" to your favorite charity because of the low basis. This way, you can avoid paying capital gains taxes, and the charity will get the full fair market value of the holding, as they avoid the capital gains taxes as well. In order to do this, you need to give the holding directly, versus selling it and then gifting the cash proceeds. If you sell the holding first, then you will have to pay the taxes, which will lower the gift amount.

4. *Yourself:* You should hold on to "Bond Mutual Fund #2" for yourself because this holding is at a loss. This means you invested more money into the fund that it is worth now. You should either keep the holding or sell it and recognize the capital loss, which you can't do if you gift it.

Outside of a cash gift—which your child may use for whatever they see fit or some agreed-upon purchase such as a down payment on a house or wedding expenses—there are a few other common ways to gift money to your children, as shown below.

To decide how to best gift the money, you need to consider how you want the child to benefit from your gift. Is the gift's intention to be strictly used for college savings? Or do you just want to provide the child with general savings to jump-start their adult lives?

Education savings:

- **529 Account:** A very common tool for saving money specifically for college education use is the 529 plan. Contributions to this plan can be made by parents, grandparents, family friends, etc., and provide a form of tax-free growth for college education. These accounts allow for a much larger annual contribution.
- **Coverdell ESA:** Coverdell education savings accounts are another form of college savings. A big plus for these accounts is that they can be used to help pay for private elementary and high schools. A downside to these accounts, however, is the $2,000 per year contribution limit.

Let's now explore, in more detail, gifting to a savings account that *isn't* meant solely for education expenses. In this case, I am talking about a UTMA (Uniform Transfers to Minors Account).

A **Uniform Transfers Minors Account (UTMA)** is a popular way to gift assets to your children. These assets can be used for a college education, but they can also be used in many other ways that benefit the minor. Control of the account ultimately passes to the minor once they reach a certain age, depending on the state in which you live (twenty-one in North Carolina). This allows them to use the money however they please.

Typically, UTMAs are not the most efficient way to save for your child's college education, but they are still an option. Many of the other options such as a 529 plan provide more tax incentives as well as tax-free growth because they're meant for college savings specifically, whereas a UTMA can be used for other expenses for the minor as well. These other expenses could include purchasing their first car, paying for a wedding, or just a general gift.

So how does a UTMA account work? Why use it over your personal investment account? The earnings in this UTMA account are taxed at the child's tax rate. Therefore, the first $1,000 of earnings is tax-free, and then the next $1,000 of earnings is taxed at 10 percent. So far so good, as that is likely much lower than what your investment account is being taxed at. What about earning over $2,000? This is where the so-called "Kiddie Tax" comes into play. This effectively means that any earnings over $2,000 will be taxed at the parents' rate.

Keep in mind that the rates mentioned apply to the *earnings*, which would include things like capital gains distributions and dividends. The actual growth of the investment returns is not taxed until you sell the fund you are invested in. This would create a long-term capital gain, which would be taxed in the year the gain was realized. However, if you were to minimize your trading in the account and realize very few gains, you could leave the funds in the account until the minor reached the age when the account would belong to them. At this point, the child could realize the gains at their tax rate, which could potentially be 0 percent, since as of 2016, those in the 10 to 15 percent tax bracket have 0 percent capital gains tax. I could see this coming in handy if you planned on assisting your child with a down payment on their first home. You could start the UTMA account when they are young and possibly have over ten years of growth that potentially could be tax-free upon the sale of the holdings outside of earnings above $2,000.

Overall, the UTMA account can be especially effective if you have gifting aspirations beyond college expenses. For the sole purpose of saving for college, though, the 529 account is likely going to be a better option, but a UTMA is certainly worth looking into, depending on your personal situation.

The Impact of Gifting

Throughout your life, you may come into situations where a friend or family member is in need of a financial gift, or maybe you just are in a position where you would like to make a generous gift to them. In that situation, you need to first determine whether your financial situation allows you to make such a gift. You must consider the impact that gifting an amount today will have on your financial situation down the road.

While you may be able to gift a relatively large amount now, will you have to adjust your future lifestyle as a result? Or does making a gift now increase the likelihood that the beneficiary of your gift will begin to expect this as an annual occurrence? Maybe you will get in the habit of wanting to make this gift annually. The first couple of years, this may seem doable, but what happens down the road, when your financial situation may be different? Will you be able to lower your gifts or eliminate them altogether?

So now that you have considered the impacts of gifting, let's say that you have decided to move forward with the gift. As of 2016, there is a $14,000 annual gift limit to each individual. This means that annual gifting under this amount doesn't have to be reported on a tax return or have any tax implications. This $14k amount reflects the limit on each person, and for a married couple, the limit doubles to $28k using gift splitting. For example, a single filer could gift up to $14k to an unlimited amount of people with no tax implications. If this single filer were married, they could gift up to $28k to the same individuals with no tax implications.

What happens if you end up making a gift larger than this annual limitation? There is actually no immediate consequence that year. Instead, any amount that goes over the annual limitation goes toward your lifetime estate tax exemption, which, as of this writing, is $5.43 million. Each year, you must file an IRA form 709 with your taxes to track your gifts made over the annual limitation. Depending on your situation, this lifetime exemption of $5.43 million (double for married couples) may never actually come into play for you, but for some, this is something to take into consideration when making gifts.

There are actually a few ways to get around the annual gift limitation. For example, you can pay the gift directly to the provider for the benefit of the giftee. An example of this would be paying directly for medical expenses or college tuition. If you make the gift directly to the medical provider or the institution, it isn't considered a gift, so it doesn't count toward the annual limit.

Overall, if you plan to make periodic gifts, you should have a financial plan in place to ensure that your gifting fits with the rest of your financial plan and that you are gifting in the most efficient way for yourself and the beneficiary. Most financial situations are constantly evolving, and you may not be able to make the same gift you made previously. Therefore, you should assess your current standing before making each periodic gift.

Charitable Gifting

If you find yourself charitably inclined, you probably have written checks to a local or national charity as a form of cash contribution. This is quite common, as most charitable contributions I see are cash donations, tangible items, or volunteering time and service. In many cases, giving in these forms makes sense, but there is another way to gift to these charities in a way that provides a benefit to you *and* the receiving charity.

While the most common gift strategy outside of cash would be the stock gifting that we just discussed, there are other items that you can gift to charity. These would include much larger, more complex assets such as a house or a portion of the proceeds from selling a business. There are also complex trust situations in which you can retain income from the trust with the remainder going to a charity upon your death.

You can even set up an investment account specifically for the purpose of gifting to charity called a Donor Advised Fund. In this instance, you make a contribution to this Donor Advised Fund, and then, in the future, you can direct funds from this account to various charities.

My goal for mentioning some of these more complex charitable strategies is not to provide the ins and outs of each, but just to raise awareness about the many options and how gifting, if important to you, should be considered a part of your overall financial plan. Although this advice may not apply to you now, it may become relevant in the future, in which case, I'd encourage you to explore these charitable gifting options further as a piece of your overall financial plan.

CHAPTER 5

FAMILY & COLLEGE PLANNING

Retirement planning can seem daunting, but at least many people have access to a retirement plan through their employer, and many even have an employer matching program that will help pad the savings on the road to retirement. But what about paying for college?

The prospect is daunting in its own right and typically doesn't come with the helpful reminder from your employer to have a little bit taken out of your paycheck each pay period so that you can build up some savings. With college savings, it's all up to you. You have to be the one to decide that now is the time to start saving for college and you have to find a way to do so.

The pressure surrounding the act of saving for and paying for college can be so overwhelming that many people never put anything away at all. Some feel it's so overwhelming that they aren't even going to try, and their child is just going to have to be saddled with student loan debt if they want to go to college.

For those who do want to pay for some or all of their children's college education, many just don't know how. This unknown is what I want to try to help you navigate. It is hard enough with one child, and harder yet for the many families who are saving for the college education of *more than one* child.

Is College the Right Choice?

I've recently heard from various podcasts I listen to, especially entrepreneurial-minded ones, that college may not provide the benefits it once did. With so many ways to consume knowledge and many avenues through which you can start your own business nowadays, is paying the rapidly increasing expense for a college education the best choice? Even if you aren't paying for all of your child's education, is thousands of dollars of student loan debt worth a college education?

In short, I will say that I believe college is still worth the financial burden, but I want to make the point that college should not be an automatic choice. This is something that you and your child should consider as a discussion point before making the final decision on whether to pursue a college education.

When you are in the process of deciding if this is a good decision or not, make sure you take all information into account. There are many ways to pay for college beyond just "out of pocket." You also need to consider that the listed sticker price you see isn't always the price that you are going to pay. Many schools give merit-based or need-based scholarships that can help ease the financial burden. This is especially the case with high price tag private schools. Even the IRS can provide some relief. Many people are eligible for the American Opportunity Tax Credit or the Lifetime Learning Credit. These tax credits can help you save a little extra on the cost of college, as they can be used when completing your tax return.

There are also many tax-advantaged accounts that are either meant for college savings or can be used for college savings. Throughout this chapter, we will explore some of these as we go on a journey of planning and paying for college.

The Cost of College

It's been over ten years since my family and I set off on my college-choosing adventure. In the span of a week, we traveled from the coast to the mountains and visited eight colleges and universities across North Carolina. It was spring break of my junior year of high school, and I was in search of my future university. The majority of these schools were public and ranged in enrollment size from about 5,000 to 30,000. Each had its own unique advantages and disadvantages compared to the other schools on the list. For example, the University of North Carolina at Wilmington didn't have a football team (priorities, I know) but was close to the beach. Appalachian State had a beautiful campus nestled in the mountains, but man, do they have some cold winters! Then there were the various amenities and academic programs each one offered.

I had a detailed spreadsheet to help me organize my likes and dislikes of each school, including their academics and amenities. This list included things such as average class size, distance from home, total enrollment, dorm life, meal plan options, and whether I could have a car on campus as a freshman, among many others.

My parents also had a detailed spreadsheet. However, theirs looked much different than mine. Their list was highlighted by tuition cost, average GPA and SAT scores for incoming freshmen, expected financial aid, scholarship opportunities, the overall likelihood of me getting into each college, and how to pay for it.

College is certainly a large expense, and it is often a goal of parents to completely cover that expense—or at least pay for a portion of it—for their children. This is usually where things get a little tricky in the financial planning for the family.

Pre-college, parents cover the everyday expenses for their children. When they are young, this might include childcare expenses. I mention childcare specifically because, in many parts of the United States, one year of full-time daycare costs more than one year of college. So, what happens between daycare and college?

Between kindergarten and senior year of high school, costs usually drop (assuming your kids go to public school) with the decrease of daycare or after-school care. So, what if we just took a percentage of what was going to daycare and put it towards savings for a college education, as well as savings toward your own retirement? Seems to me that you could split it up into thirds and move some to college savings, some to retirement, and the remainder to your children's activities, and therefore, all goals are met.

More commonly, what I see is that after daycare expenses end, parents just improve their lifestyle and go buy a new car or spend extra on themselves since they now have that extra surplus. This continues for multiple years until the parents hear a college planning commercial on the radio and think, "Maybe I should start saving for my child's college education." While there may still potentially be enough time to save, it is often very difficult for the parents to cut back the lifestyle they are now accustomed to so that they can save for the college education.

Paying for It

As of 2016, Americans owe more than $1.26 trillion in student loan debt with an average balance per graduating student of about $37,000 owed.[20] This seemingly increases every year, with 2016 numbers up 6 percent from 2015.

I've noticed a distinct trend when discussing college planning with clients in their thirties with young children. Many of them, prior to meeting me, have already started a college savings plan such as a 529 account, and have begun putting a couple hundred dollars in the account each month. Through our conversations, I can tell that college planning for their children is high on their priority list and in many cases a more pressing topic to them than their own long-term savings and financial future.

It's also pretty interesting to see the client paying off their own student loans at a couple hundred dollars a month and simultaneously contributing to their child's 529 account in the same manner. They express that their own student loans have delayed their desire to buy a house or max out their Roth IRA, or the loans have just generally been a weight they drag around. If they can help it, they don't want their children to have to experience the same feelings of being saddled with student loan debt as they start their post-college lives. Therefore, college planning is a key goal and priority for them in the realm of their whole financial plan.

So how do these parents go about thinking and planning for a college education for their children? Well, once the decision has been made about who is going to pay for school—or a combination of who is going to pay for school, such as parents and grandparents—then you can decide on what investment vehicles and strategies you can use to most efficiently pay for the education.

What if you decide that the best way for you to help your children or grandchildren pay for college is to simply write them a check so they can pay for it themselves? I'm sure they would have no problem with that, as they could just turn around and pay the college tuition themselves. However, is this the most efficient way to do this? As you've seen previously in chapter four, gifting cash is usually not the most efficient way to gift money. If you were still to decide that this is the best option for you, then you would be restricted by the annual gift limit in order not to eat into your lifetime limit.

When it comes to college expenses, though, you can avoid the annual gift limit altogether. The way you do this is instead of writing a check made out to the student as a gift, just write the check directly to the school. This way, the annual gift limit doesn't come into consideration. You can actually do this with medical expenses as well.

Also in chapter four, I discussed gifting to your children or grandchildren and touched on different ways to do so, including a 529 account and a Coverdell ESA account. In that chapter, we limited our discussion to the basics, outlining potential routes you could choose if you intended your gift to be put toward college. Now I want to dive a little deeper into how a parent or grandparent can truly help the child pay for college.

529 Account

The 529 account is the most common vehicle I see when it comes to saving for college. Typically, the parents (but many times the grandparents) open an account and make contributions for the child. These contributions can then be invested and grow tax-free until needed to cover college expenses. As long as the distributions are used for qualified expenses, there are no taxes or penalties on the distributions.

When making these contributions, there are some things to keep in mind. Let's say you open the account yourself and begin contributions. The annual gift tax limit ($14k in 2017) applies, and you will need to stay under that for your annual contribution without eating into your lifetime estate tax limit. 529 accounts also have another option that will allow you to contribute more than the annual limit. In this case, you can make a much larger up-front lump sum contribution that would be the equivalent of the next five years. I like this feature, as it gives you five more years of being invested and eligible for the tax-free growth. In this second option, you won't be able to contribute again within those first five years if you make the maximum contribution that first year.

A 529 account owned by a grandparent does have some different rules opposed to one owned by the parent that affect the child's potential to receive federal student aid. The 529 account itself is not considered an asset owned by the student, so it doesn't have any impact on the financial aid. However, a portion of distributions from the grandparent-owned 529 account is considered income to the student in regard to aid.

Gifting Appreciated Stock

Gifting appreciated stock can be done as a generic gift but can also be used as a gift to the child to help them pay for college. This is especially attractive if you are in a high tax bracket but the child would be in a low tax bracket and could avoid any kiddie tax. The reason for this is that the cost basis of the stock that you hold carries over to the child. Therefore, when they sell the stock to pay for school, the child is responsible for capital gains incurred, if any.

Pay Directly

Maybe the most obvious and potentially simplest way would be to just pay the school directly. In doing so, you could pay the tuition bill directly each semester. The advantage of this is that the annual gift tax limit does not apply if you are paying the school directly. However, it can only be for tuition and not for other education-related expenses.

Overall, there are certainly ways to help pay for your child's education, but you have to determine what's best for you and your family's situation, as some avenues may be more advantageous than others.

Roth IRA

When it comes to saving for your children's college education in a savings account that is not education-specific, look no further than the Roth IRA. While typically associated with retirement savings, this account can be used for paying for your children's education as well.

Saving in a Roth IRA can help you save for retirement and college at the same time. This option tends to work nicely for those individuals who may not have the extra cash flow to save in a 529 account or pay for college out of pocket. If the child ends up either not going to college or not getting enough scholarships and financial aid, then you would just continue to use the Roth IRA for retirement savings. If you do end up needing to use the Roth IRA account to cover your child's college education, then you can pull out the contributions from the Roth IRA to pay for college.

As you can see, there are a number of different ways to go about paying for college, and the best one will depend on your current financial situation as well as where the child wants to go to school. Especially with private schools, you will find that the sticker price of the cost to attend won't always end up being what you pay, given the opportunities for scholarships and financial aid.

During each year of your child attending school, you may want to use a variation of strategies to pay for college. You may pay a certain amount of the tuition from your cash savings instead of the 529 account in order to make sure you are eligible for any tax credits available. Or, depending on your financial aid situation, you may want to wait until later in the student's college career to use grandparent-funded education accounts.

Ultimately, gifting in any way to your children or grandchildren to fund their college education can be a great way to help them during this transition period of their lives as they consider what to study and the impact they want to have on the world.

CHAPTER 6

FAMILY & TAX PLANNING

I believe that tax planning is the honey hole of financial planning, as just about every topic we have talked about and every topic we will discuss throughout this book is impacted by taxes.

Before I get too far into this chapter, there is one thing you should recognize upfront, and that is the line you have heard many times over the years: "The only things certain in life are death and taxes." There is also a line from a song I enjoy by country singer Tracy Lawrence: "I got that Friday paycheck in my hand, minus a bite from Uncle Sam, but no complaints, I understand it's the nature of the game."

In summary, you can't escape the fact that you will owe taxes on income you make. However, there are a multitude of ways to implement tax-efficient strategies so that you do not pay more taxes than you have to. This takes a little more effort than just setting your withholdings through payroll with your employer at the beginning of each year and then hoping things work out come April 15 when you've completed your tax return.

Tax planning is a continuous aspect of your finances and should be monitored throughout the year with short-term and long-term effects kept in mind when making financial decisions. As you may have noticed, taxes seem to infiltrate every area of your financial planning life. I want to provide a summary guide of other areas from this book to watch out for when planning so that you can remain as tax efficient as possible.

American Opportunity Tax Credit (AOTC)

In order to claim this credit for college expenses, your Modified Adjusted Gross Income (MAGI) must be under $90,000 if a single filer and under $180,000 if married filing jointly (as of 2016). Along with meeting these MAGI limits, you will need to pay $4,000 worth of college education expenses out of pocket, versus from an education account such as a 529. In doing so, you can receive up to a $2,500 tax credit.

Student Loan Interest

To qualify for at least a partial deduction, you will need to have an Adjusted Gross Income (AGI) of less than $80,000 if single and less than $160,000 if married filing jointly.

Gifting

As we discussed in the gifting chapter, when gifting stock to your children, you should not gift any holdings that you have with unrealized losses. This is because you wouldn't be able to realize the loss and report it on your tax return. In this situation, you would be better off realizing the loss for your tax return and then gifting the cash from the sale of that holding.

Uniform Transfer to Minors Act (UTMA)

In the gifting chapter, we touched on gifting to your family—specifically your children—but now, I want to dive into greater detail about the tax benefits of some of these gifting strategies.

I recently met with a client who was interested in lowering their tax liability and brought up the desire to gift to their children as well. Specifically, they desired to provide their kids with resources to attend a high-quality private high school. Here is where an application of a UTMA account can come into play. If the client annually contributes to the UTMA account for each of their children with the purpose of paying for their future education, they will be able to save taxes on the account earnings. This works because UTMA accounts are taxed under the "Kiddie Tax" rules, and therefore, the earnings on the account won't be taxed at the parents' rate until earnings exceed $2,000. Whereas, if they had left the funds in their personal investment account, they would be liable for taxes on all the earnings, not just those over $2,000.

These UTMA accounts also work well if the child does, in fact, have funds available in the account after they graduate from college. This is because any gains in the account are taxed at the child's rate at this point, which may allow for the 0 percent capital gains rate if they are in a low enough tax bracket. So, all the funds that have been growing in their UTMA can be sold, and gains realized with zero tax liability can be used for a house down payment, graduate school, or any other expenses that they need to cover at the time.

Sale of a Business

I recently attended a conference on the topic of finances and giving called "Plan to Give."[21] The nature of this conference allowed for us to dive deep into complex charitable gifting strategies and think outside the box, beyond the more common ways of cash gifting.

For example, did you know you can gift part of your business ownership before you sell? Say you planned to sell your business, and with the proceeds, you planned to have a nice retirement, but you also planned to give some to charity after the sale. In this case, you would usually write the check to the charity straight from your bank account. But what if I told you there was a more efficient way to donate that would provide greater benefits to both you and the charity? If you were to gift a portion of the equity of your company to an intermediary such as a Donor Advised Fund, then you could reduce capital gains tax on the sale. Plus, this allows you to get a business tax deduction for charitable gifting, which would lower your overall tax liability. Giving the charitable gift before you sell the company allows you to be more tax efficient as well as allowing a larger gift to be made to the charity compared to waiting until after the net sale proceeds.

There are many other ways to integrate tax efficiency into your family's financial goals, so be sure to explore how your financial decisions can be conducted in the most tax efficient way before the end of a tax year. You may be able to defer more income to your 401(k), for example, in order to lower your AGI enough to take advantage of some of these deductions and credits. Also, keep in mind that some of these examples may not apply to you depending on your specific tax situation, but I have found a number of them to be helpful over the years.

CHAPTER 7

SHARING & PLANNING WITH YOUR CHILDREN

M oney, politics and religion are those topics we should supposedly avoid, especially with our families—
subjects where we all have our own personal viewpoints and would offend or make things awkward if we were to
discuss them with others.

Nearly half of Americans say that the most challenging topic to
discuss with others is personal finances (44 percent). Compare
that to the topics that rank as *less* difficult: death (38 percent),
politics (35 percent), religion (32 percent), taxes (21 percent),
and personal health (20 percent). These results come from
Wells Fargo's Financial Health study[22], a national online survey
conducted by Market Probe, Inc. of 1,004 adults between the
ages of twenty-five and seventy-five, designed to take the pulse
of Americans' perceptions of their own financial health.

Karen Wimbish, director of Retail Retirement at Wells Fargo, states, "It's not surprising people don't want to talk about money, investments, tax strategies, or even how much to put aside for a child's education. But not spending time today to think about the future can be costly in the long-run. I think of personal finance in the same vein as my health—I wouldn't keep concerns about my physical health private. I'd consult a doctor or talk to a friend or family member about it."

Seventy-one percent of adults surveyed learned the importance of saving from their own parents. Despite this, only a third (36 percent) of today's parents report discussing the importance of saving money with their children frequently, with 64 percent indicating that they talk about savings with their kids less than weekly or never.

Well, as a financial planner, I get to talk about money a lot, and by "a lot," I mean all day long. The thing is, though, I'm not talking about *my* money or *my* finances: I have to ask other people, often whom I've just met, about their own finances and financial goals.

During my initial client meetings, I always spend a good bit of time data gathering so that I can understand the financial issues that led them to contact me in the first place. My goal is to get below the surface and discover the true driving factor behind their desire to "organize" their finances or determine if they are on the right track for retirement.

I'll often uncover answers such as "I don't know what I'm doing. I have never had a plan for my finances. I make a good income, but after throwing a little bit to my employer's 401(k), I still feel like I'm squeezed each month." Or, "I want to be able to retire at age sixty. I watched my parents work until they were seventy-five because they had to. I want to learn from that and prepare to be in a financial situation where I only have to work because I want to and not because I have to."

Nearly 100 percent of the time, there seems to be a driving factor behind why clients contact me. They then schedule a meeting to come discuss their finances with some young guy they have never met. I have rarely found that clients were afraid to share their finances with me, including income, account balances, tax returns, or even their expenses and what they spend most of their money on. I essentially get to see their finances presented as an open book.

So, if they are so quick to share their financial information with me the first time we ever meet, why are they so hesitant to share this with their children? Are they embarrassed? Do they not want to have to explain themselves for decisions they have made? Or maybe they think that their child won't work as hard, as they may anticipate an inheritance?

Whatever the reason, the facts show that 50 percent of baby boomers have *never* engaged in conversations with their children about money. This is especially puzzling to me when these clients are often "sandwiched" between caring for their elderly parents while also raising their children. They will usually say something along the lines of, "I think my parents are okay financially. I don't really know, but they haven't mentioned anything about it. I sure wish I could know so that if I need to help them financially I can plan to do so while I juggle sending my kids to college and saving for retirement myself."

These individuals want to know about their parents' financial situations so that they can plan their own finances in case they need to help their parents financially at some point. So wouldn't it make sense for these individuals to learn from this and therefore share financial information with their children, so they don't go through this same problem?

How do you go through this process, though? Where do you start? I've come up with a three-step process to approach this discussion, which pertains to college-aged children and younger.

1. How are your children going to handle this new information? You know your child better than anyone, so you know if they are mature enough to have this conversation with you. You

know if you may need to be patient and bring this topic along slowly. This could particularly be the case if you have never put an emphasis on teaching your children about money and how to handle it. On the other hand, if you have been planting seeds all along the way, you may be able to more quickly and easily have this discussion with your children.

2. Don't get too specific at first. You want to provide your child with an idea of your financial situation, but don't feel the need to bring out your account statements and go line by line. That is too much too soon! You want to share the larger picture, which will likely provoke your child to ask their own questions.

3. A good time to discuss this with your children can be when they get their first job that has benefits. They get that first 401(k) enrollment application and don't know what to do. Who do you think they are going to turn to? Well, maybe you hope it is you, but maybe they turn to their friend or coworker first. Is that really who you want them taking financial advice from? Take this time to teach and share with them your knowledge and experience of your retirement accounts.

It's not just helping them set up their 401(k). It's incorporating this financial lesson in all aspects of your life. When you purchase a new home or a new car, pay a credit card bill, or take action for some financial purpose, take that opportunity to plant a little seed regarding your approach to handling money. This will open the door for your child to ask her or his own questions when ready, through which you can get a feel for their thought process about handling money.

Sharing Your Financial Situation with Your Adult Children

You've spent your whole life teaching your children various skills: how to walk, tie their shoes, throw a baseball, drive a car, apply for their first job, obtain a mortgage for their first house— the list goes on and on. These teachings have gotten them to where they are today, and as they are now grown, maybe your discussions with them have changed. While you will always be "teaching" them as they seek your guidance, you may find yourself starting to learn from *them*, as they are now grown adults themselves.

Your conversations with them may change and become more in-depth about careers, family situations, most recent happenings in the news, and even finances. This is where you start to recognize that the seeds you planted years ago about how to handle finances have (hopefully) sprouted, and you can see what they have grown into. If you sense that your children are ready to discuss financial matters with you, then I recommend you proceed.

1. Don't be afraid to share your mistakes and failures.

It has been my experience that opening up about personal mistakes or items you wish you had done differently helps create a trusting, open space to share your financial viewpoints and encourage your adult child to contribute their views as well. Think back to when you were their age. What would you have done differently if you could go back? Did you unnecessarily learn something the hard way? What can you do to improve the financial future of your child? Overall, you are looking for stories that you can share that will resonate with them for years to come.

2. Don't be afraid to share your successes.

Just as you shouldn't shy away from your failures, you should also share your successes. In doing so, I don't mean you brag or pressure your child to do the exact same thing. I'm talking about sharing successes in ways that will help and encourage them to be proactive with their finances. Walk them through how you got your first job, made your first successful investment, or started your own company, and share how you took the leap of faith needed to do so. Share the struggles but also share the successes and how you got to where you are today.

Parents, Kids, and Money

T. Rowe Price does an annual study titled "Parents, Kids, and Money Survey."[23] 2016 marked the eighth year of the repeated study, and a number of the results surprised me. For example, 51 percent of parents surveyed said that a Roth IRA is a way to save for retirement where you contribute pre-tax money! Obviously, there is still an education gap when it comes to investing, as only 35 percent of those surveyed correctly responded that Roth IRA contributions are made with *after-tax* money.

Immediately following this section of the study was a series of questions about discussing finances with children. The first question, "How often do you discuss any financial topics with your kids?" is pretty easily answered, with 87 percent saying they do discuss topics with their kids. Results ranged from once a day or a few times a week to once a month or less. So far, so good, with the vast majority discussing financial topics with their children. However, what happens when the questions get a little more personal?

For example, consider the results of this question: "How reluctant are you to discuss financial matters with your kids?" Think about this for yourself for a minute. Are you reluctant at all to discuss finances with your children? According to the study, 71 percent state that they are, in fact, reluctant to some degree to discuss financial matters with their children.

At first, this 71 percent may seem high, but I don't think that is the case, as it seems to have more to do with the knowledge and confidence the parent has in financial matters themselves— which, given the earlier example of the Roth IRA question, may not be a high number. In fact, when comparing the level of comfort in discussing finances as well as other potentially uncomfortable topics, only sex and death surveyed as being more uncomfortable discussions than finances. Not too surprising there, but consider that discussing financial matters was more comfortable than other topics such as drugs, bullying, and terrorism. Because of the reluctance and discomfort, only 15 percent of those surveyed set aside specific time to discuss financial topics with their kids with the remainder only discussing these topics if they come up.

In summary, this study demonstrates the general notion that we don't like to discuss money and finances with others, even our children. So how do we change that course of action so that we can help our family increase their financial knowledge and prepare them for their financial future? In the following pages, I'll outline the eight steps I believe you can take to talk to your children and family members about finances. This outline starts with basic steps to implement when children are young, and proceeds to more complicated financial matters worth discussing with young adults and eventually, adult children.

Before I continue, however, let me say one more thing. I know that some of you are going to think of several reasons *not* to discuss finances with your children, especially in regard to your personal situation, including the potential inheritance you may leave behind. While there are some criteria that may support this notion (as mentioned previously) there are likely situations where you should be communicating with your children, as long as they are responsible and mature enough to hear it.

So what is really hindering you from talking with your children about money? Are you worried about how they will react when they discover they may be receiving an inheritance? After all, you don't want your children to come to expect and plan for the inheritance. This could lead to them coasting their way through school and not taking their careers seriously because they are expecting a lump sum of money later in life. If this is the case, then it is important to ask yourself: "What can I proactively do to teach my children how to handle an inheritance?" What measures can you take prior to and after they learn of an inheritance they may be receiving?

1. Start as early as possible. As I've already discussed, laying that foundation as early as possible is key to making sure your children don't implement bad financial habits.

2. Slowly teach them financial basics such credit cards. Teach them that just because you can get a free T-shirt for signing up for a credit card at the student union doesn't make it the best decision. Or when they have a large car maintenance expense and it completely wipes out their savings account, share tips on how to build back up their savings.

3. Let them experience investing for themselves first. The best place for this is likely the 401(k) at their first job out of college. Let them feel what it is like to save a portion of their paycheck for long-term investing. Let them make mistakes early on with their investments and learn lessons that will stick with them throughout their investing lives.

4. Instill the importance of savings habits. The best place for them to learn savings habits is by seeing their parents' habits. While they won't see the exact numbers of your savings, you can mention how you allocate your money, just like you did as a child when you had a piggy bank for savings, spending, and charity.

5. Share a little about your situation. I think a good place to start would be when your child is getting started on their own 401(k). You could mention what it was like for you when you started your first 401(k). Share if and how your thoughts have changed regarding the role the 401(k) plays in the retirement portfolio. Tell them what you wish you would have known when you were their age, given what you know now.

6. Observe how they react to the tidbits of your financial situation that you shared. What was their first response? Did they seem inquisitive about the whole thing, or did they make some comment about the inheritance they hope to get? To me, if they ask thoughtful questions about your plans for your financial future and how you got to that point, it shows a mature adult who is ready for the responsibility of prudently managing their money as well as any future inheritance.

7. Explain that inheritance isn't guaranteed and potentially share an example about your parents. If you're like most people, your parents probably used up a large chunk of their finances in their later stages of life on high healthcare expenses. The point of this would be to instill the notion that your children can't count on an inheritance from you to supplement their lifestyle or their retirement savings.

8. Trust that you have set the foundation for handling money and an inheritance. At the end of the day, it will be up to them on how they choose to handle their finances. You likely won't agree with every decision they make, but trust that overall, you have provided them with the best road map you know to set them on a successful path to managing their financial matters.

CHAPTER 8

FAMILY & INSURANCE PLANNING

"What if?"

That phrase always comes to mind about when I think about insurance. We pay premiums monthly or annually and hope we never actually benefit from them. While that seems counterintuitive, it's exactly what we want to happen. We've spent the previous chapters detailing how we save and invest to align our finances with our family values, but how do we protect what we have built for the family we love if the "what if" happens?

The preceding chapters built up your financial life and helped you put in place an efficient plan to achieve your financial goals. This chapter is all about protecting everything you have worked hard to build. Up to this point in the book, we have focused on building a good offense: contributing to retirement accounts, paying for children's college education, and gifting to charities, among other items. These are all offensive strategies. On the flip side, insurance planning is like building a good defense.

There is a common saying that "defense wins championships," and this is definitely true in insurance planning. Very rarely does an athletic team win championships with only a good offense scoring lots of points. The best teams are usually more balanced and have a good offense as well as a good defense. In the same way, your financial lives should be balanced enough to not fall apart if one aspect is struggling.

With life insurance, if you were to pass, your spouse can still provide for your family with the life insurance proceeds. If you have good income and are very dependent on that consistent income, disability insurance is an important thing to have in case you are unable to work for a period of time. With disability insurance, you can still have a consistent income even if you aren't able to work at your normal job. Another piece of insurance that can be used as a good defense is long-term care insurance. This will help you cover costs if you need long-term care for medical reasons later in your life. Let's dig into each of these three items.

Life Insurance

"I pay the water bill, the electricity, the mortgage, and that policy that takes care of my family should the good Lord call my name."

This a line from a country song by Tracy Lawrence that references a life insurance policy and why he has one. He works hard to pay his monthly expenses such as the water bill, electricity, and the mortgage, but he also mentions that he is paying monthly premiums for a life insurance policy. This is what insurance is for: a defense to take care of your family and your financial situation if something were to happen to you. Life insurance makes sense for just about everyone who provides for someone else, whether that be family or others.

I often get the sense that life insurance is a touchy subject for some to talk about. Ultimately, discussing one's demise isn't on the top of most people's list of things to discuss today. However, that is always what drives someone to want to purchase life insurance: the assurance that their family will be taken care of if they were to pass.

I won't go into great detail about the many different life insurance policies out there. I could write multiple books on the ins and outs of some of the plans I've seen, given their complexity. To sum up life insurance, I'll just say that you essentially must decide if you need life insurance coverage for your whole life or just for a period of time.

When I say a "period of time," this could be ten, twenty, or thirty years in which you need the coverage. If you were to die during that time period, then the death benefit would be paid out to your beneficiaries as intended, but if you were to die after that time period, there would be no death benefit, as your policy would expire. On the other hand, you can purchase a policy that covers you for your whole life. This way, no matter when you pass, even if it's at an elderly age, your beneficiaries receive the death benefit.

Either option is viable and can be appropriate to you depending on your financial situation, but there is also an emotional decision involved. Some people may not need coverage for their entire life, but they want it, knowing that they will leave in place a financial gift to their beneficiaries upon their death.

So, what factors play a role in determining what type of life insurance is needed—or if it is needed at all? One of the most common choices I see people make is getting a term policy to cover them while their children are still minors. This could be a twenty-year term policy you get when your child is born. This way, if you were to pass, your spouse would have the financial resources to support your children with the absence of one spouse's income.

Another common choice is a term policy that expires approximately around the time you retire. At your retirement, you no longer have a salaried income that your family is relying on to pay the expenses, so if you were to pass, there would be no income lost. At this point, many people become what is called "self-insured," which means they have saved enough financial resources over their working years to cover the other spouse if they were to pass away. Therefore, it may not be advantageous to continue paying premium payments on a life insurance policy if you are self-insured. This is where the emotional decision comes into play, as they consider what kind of financial legacy they want or need to leave.

Disability Insurance

"You can hope for the best and plan for the worst. If lightning doesn't strike you first, who knows what's going to happen in the end. I just work like it's all up to me and pray like it's all up to Him."

Another line from the Tracy Lawrence song that highlights how many aspects of our life aren't always within our control. We can set up a plan for retirement and other financial aspects of our lives, but many times, "life happens," and we have to deviate from the plan.

I'm sure you regularly see ads on television or elsewhere that depict life insurance companies, showing families having a backyard cookout or sitting around the dinner table. It probably stirs your emotions on the importance of life insurance and providing for your family if you were to unexpectedly pass away. Because of this, most individuals have some kind of life insurance, whether through their employer or an out-side provider.

Disability insurance ads seem to be a lot less common. The reality is, though, that if you are twenty-five years old, you have a one in four chance of becoming disabled at some point in your life.[24] This means that either for a short or long period of time, you won't be able to work and provide income for your family. Or you may be able to work but unable to do your current job, which requires a certain skill that your disability prevents you from doing. So not only would you have no income (or a reduced income), but your expenses could potentially increase as a result of your disability. With life insurance, when you pass, household expenses would typically decrease by a certain percentage. An unexpected disability, however, creates a double-whammy, where your household income goes down but you still have to cover expenses just as you did before the disability.

Income is essential. Most of us get paid every couple of weeks and schedule our mortgage payment and other bills accordingly. We then know how much we have for other items in our life such as entertainment, shopping, or kids' activities. This works great as long as there are no huge, unexpected changes to income. One high-impact unexpected change to income occurs if we can't work at all! I'm not talking about getting fired or laid off, either. I'm talking about not being able to work because of a medical-related occurrence that prohibits working for either a semi-long-term or long-term period. This is where disability insurance comes in.

Having disability insurance is just like life insurance—you pay a monthly premium and then benefit from the insurance upon a trigger event. There are a number of disability insurance options to choose from, but ultimately, the goal is to replace a portion of your income if you are unable to work.

While I think it makes sense for just about everyone to look into getting disability insurance—especially if you have many working years left—there are some people who are *even more* in need of getting covered as soon as possible.

1. If you are the sole income earner of the family, or if you have a much higher proportionate income compared to your spouse, then the need for you to have disability insurance increases. Being the breadwinner of the family would make for a big adjustment if you weren't able to work and provide income.

2. This category is similar to the situation in example 1, but even more so for those who have very high expenditures and little accessible savings. These individuals typically make a high income but also spend at a very high level. Therefore, they don't have a lot of outside savings or even an emergency fund

that could be utilized during a time of short-term disability. They rely so heavily on the cash flow their income provides that they would be hit hard if a disability prevented them from earning that income for a period of time.

3. Individuals who work in a profession that is more prone to injury. For example, my wife is a nurse at a local hospital where she is typically on her feet for most of the day. She is in and out of patients' rooms tending to their needs and checking their vital signs to make sure they are at appropriate levels. Sometimes, there is a need to assist the patient in walking or getting in and out of bed, and depending on their condition, patients usually lean their weight on the nurses to help balance themselves. Of course, this pressure on the nurse's body can take a toll over time and lead to complications, causing the nurses not to be able to do their jobs in the future. For people in fields such as these, in which a certain level of physical activity is required, the need for disability insurance increases.

As you approach retirement, the need for disability insurance likely will decline, depending on your personal situation. With fewer working years left, a disability won't affect your financial situation as much if you are unable to work or have to take a lower paying job, especially if you have saved up a large enough nest egg that you could tap it if forced into early retirement.

Long-Term Care Insurance (LTC)

One of the most common fears I hear from those just about to enter retirement is, "I don't want to have to be a financial burden on my adult children or other family members during my later retirement years."

In this sense, they want to make sure that when they choose to retire, they will have enough financial resources to support their lifestyle so that they don't have to count on someone else. We typically discuss the anticipated expenses in retirement—think back to the "smile graph" example in the Retirement Planning chapter—where spending is high just after retirement, decreases towards the middle and later years of your retirement, and rises again with the uptick towards the later years of your life.

The tail end of the smile is where long-term care insurance comes into play. The average annual cost for an assisted living facility in North Carolina as of 2016 was $36,000 per person![25] This number likely comes as a shock to you unless you have had a parent or relative go through an extended care facility. So how do you plan for this? In most cases, you have three options:

1. Income

Some of you may actually have good income during your retirement years that would go towards these medical costs. Most commonly, this would come from Social Security, pension, or even rental real estate income. Having this income in retirement creates a "floor," in which, even if you ran out of assets, you would at least have this base level of income each year.

2. Savings

Since pensions aren't as common now as they previously were, many of you likely only have Social Security to count on as income in retirement. Given that most Social Security amounts aren't going to be enough to cover your lifestyle expenses, let alone any long-term care, you will need to supplement your income through your personal savings to cover expenses. This is where the term "nest egg" comes into play. During your working years, you diligently save in your company's 401(k) plan or other investment vehicle in hopes that you will save up enough so that when you retire, you will be able to live comfortably on your savings. This is why saving during your working years in a 401(k), Roth IRA, and/or other savings methods is so important, as these savings will be crucial to your retirement years.

3. Long-Term Care Insurance

Another option that is meant specifically to cover those extended medical needs typically later in life is long-term care insurance. This is a type of insurance similar to disability insurance. While disability insurance works well while you are still employed, in case you can't work for a period of time, long-term care insurance is typically reserved until a need for assisted living or another form of extended care is needed.

So how do you know if long-term care insurance is right for you? Depending on your personal situation, you may not need long-term care insurance. If you have a high floor as we discussed earlier, with pension or Social Security income plus some saved personal assets, you may be able to cover the cost of long-term care and therefore not have to pay for the premiums. Another situation where you may not need the insurance could be if you have a large enough nest egg that your assets would be sufficient to cover you and your spouse if you needed care later on in retirement. This situation would commonly be referred to as self-insured.

So what if neither of the above situations really fits your personal situation? Or maybe you are feeling like that Stealers Wheel song, "Stuck in the Middle with You," and you have a small pension and some saved assets, but are not sure that it would be enough to cover you in the event of a long-term care need. This scenario would make you a good candidate for long-term care insurance, especially if you were able to afford the premiums. With a small pension and some saved assets, if your spouse were to go into long-term care, they would use up a large portion of your assets. Then, upon their death, you would be left with little to support yourself. Having long-term care insurance prevents that situation.

Determine which of these three funding options fits your situation financially and provides you with the peace of mind that your assets can cover unexpected medical expenses as well as leave a legacy if desired.

CHAPTER 9

FAMILY & ESTATE PLANNING

J ust about every person should have some sort of estate plan in place. However, this is often one of the most procrastinated areas of a financial plan, in my experience. I find this odd, especially for people such as many of you reading this book, who seem to be focused on family-centric financial planning strategies.

The most common reason for this procrastination I see is the difficulty of thinking about and planning for one's own death or incapacity. While it's true that estate planning mostly centers on this scenario, there are a few other areas of estate planning that can be triggered or become relevant while one is still living. Just as disability insurance is often forgotten about after life insurance, in estate planning, power of attorney can often be an afterthought behind a last will and testament. Throughout this chapter, we will look at different estate planning ideas and how they apply to the stage of life you may be in.

Each stage of our lives is accompanied by different demands, needs, and desires. In college, we need a few bucks to go to Bojangles' for a four-piece supreme dinner. We then move into the next stage of our lives in search for a job to provide income for our basic needs. Likely, a small apartment will do, and a car just to get us from point A to B. Then, as our lives evolve, we may get married or have children, changing our needs from a small one-bedroom apartment to a larger home and a more reliable car. The list of changes goes on and on, but the point is, your needs are dependent on your current life situation.

This is no different when it comes to estate planning. Let's take a look at different items that may be relevant for you to think about, depending on what stage of life you are in.

Early Career with No Children

If you are single or newly married with no children, then you may not have a will or any other estate documents. While you may think that you do not need formal estate planning documents, since you do not have many assets, there are some estate planning documents that I would still strongly encourage you to have in place.

1. A power of attorney allows for an appointed individual to make decisions for you in the case that you are not able to do so. This could include financial or medical decisions.

2. A living will or advanced medical directive allows you to make the decision regarding sustainment of life.

If you are not in this category but have children or grandchildren who are, one thing to think about is whether you'd be able to access medical records in case of an emergency. You may not have access to your college student or young adult's medical records and may not be able to make health-related decisions for them if they are in a position where they are unable to make their own decisions. However, you and your children can complete the necessary legal documents. Your child can sign off to allow you access to these items in a time of need.

Early Career with Children

When children join a family, it is a key estate planning time for you. A few common documents to put in place at this time are:

1. Last Will and Testament
2. Power of Attorney (POA)
3. Living Will

In the will, you should have a guardian appointed for your children if you and your spouse were to pass. You can also set up a testamentary trust; upon your passing, your investment accounts would go into the trust for your beneficiaries. This is especially useful for those with children who are not yet of an age to manage their own inheritance. You can set certain rules, such as they don't receive the money until they have reached age twenty-five. Or they can only use the money for college expenses if they are under twenty-five. Even a twenty-five-year-old may not be ready to handle a large sum of money, so you could also consider making only a percentage available at twenty-five, with the remaining amount available at age thirty.

Mid-Career Job Change or Moving Around the Country

This is a good time to review and possibly update your estate documents. Chances are high that you have moved a few times since you had estate documents drafted. Therefore, the state you currently reside in may not have been the state you had the estate documents drafted in, and you should look into updating the documents to your current state of residence. Given the potential that you moved from one place to another because of a new job opportunity, you may now have multiple retirement plans from different employers. When moving to a new job, this is a good time to double-check that the beneficiaries on each account have been designated as you desire.

Divorce and Remarriage

While not applicable to all, a high percentage of the population has experienced a divorce. If this applies to you, you may have implemented an estate plan with their ex-spouse, which would need updating unless you want everything to be left to your ex-spouse. This is especially true when there are children involved from a previous marriage or if one of you has remarried and has children with a new spouse.

This is where your estate plan can get pretty complicated, and you can really make some mistakes if it is not carefully and regularly updated. You will want to make sure that all your desires for estate distribution are met. For example, you may want your child from a previous marriage to be included in your estate plan, but not the parent (ex-spouse) of that child. You will need to lay this out in your estate plan to include the child but not the ex-spouse, all while considering your current spouse and, potentially, children you've had or will have with them.

Also, think about the beneficiaries on your retirement plans. Leaving an ex-spouse as a beneficiary after a divorce, depending on the relationship, may be your preferred beneficiary status, but what happens if you remarry? Would you want your ex-spouse to receive your inheritance over your current spouse?

Retirement Age

When you retire, take some time to really lock down your estate plan. While you are working through your retirement administrative duties, this is a good time to coordinate your estate plan with the updated changes in your life instead of waiting five years when you are in "retirement mode" and may not have the drive or are just out of practice with paperwork and documents such as this.

1. Consider estate planning while you can still make your own decisions.

2. Establish a team of experts to work with your children if necessary upon your death. This team would usually consist of an attorney, a financial planner, and an accountant.

3. This is also a good time, if you have not already done so, to fill others in on your estate planning desires and where they can find this information if you were to pass. This should be shared with those close to you, especially your designated beneficiaries.

Your Beneficiaries

In the book *The Legacy Journey*[26], Dave Ramsey makes an interesting point about sharing your estate plan with your beneficiaries. He wasn't necessarily referring to assets but was more focused on general everyday financial obligations and details that would assist others in taking care of your estate if you were to pass. These things include utility bills, insurance information for home or auto, where to find keys to a lock box, among many other items. Typically, these aren't things you would find in official estate documents but are other items that would be helpful for beneficiaries to have in the event of your death. In his book, Ramsey mentions that leaving your beneficiaries a highly organized paperwork trail, and clear instructions for all aspects of your finances and estate, is one of the best gifts you could give them at that time.

Beneficiary Mishaps

You know that form you were given when you started at your current job and enrolled in the 401(k) plan? Yeah, the one where you chose who your beneficiaries for your retirement account would be. Remember how quickly you could write in your spouse's name, their date of birth, and other pertinent information? Ensuring that the correct beneficiaries are on your retirement accounts is really one of the easiest and most impactful estate planning moves you can make. Even updating this after the initial setup can often be done quickly online or with a simple form through your Human Resources department.

But if it's so easy, then why do so many of the new clients I meet with have incomplete or outdated beneficiaries on their retirement accounts? With the complexity of clients' financial situations and potentially numerous old 401(k)s, I can see how this can happen, especially when some of those old 401(k)s were started before they were even married. However, no matter the explanation for forgetting to update beneficiaries, this really is a key and simple area that must be periodically checked for accuracy.

You may be reading this and thinking, "Not me. I would never forget to put beneficiaries on my accounts, and I always updated them when my children were born or other life events occurred." Let me share with you some common mishaps I've seen.

1. Outdated beneficiary information on 401(k)s. If you started your job before you were married, before your children were born, or before a divorce, did you change that beneficiary information after those events? If you had no dependents when you started, your beneficiary might be your parents or a sibling. Typically, I see a change over to the spouse as the primary beneficiary upon marriage, but if you were to unexpectedly pass before you switched the beneficiary, your spouse would not receive anything.

2. Selecting a primary beneficiary, but failing to designate a contingent beneficiary. The contingent beneficiary is typically children or another non-spouse beneficiary. With minor children, this is where the testamentary trust in your will can be used.

How to Leave an Inheritance

"A good man leaves an inheritance to his children's children." —Proverbs 13:22[27]

In your investment accounts, there are strategies you should make sure you take advantage of when passing along assets. One, for example, is if you have a taxable brokerage account that may have large, unrealized gains in it. Often, late in life, an individual wants to make a gift to their beneficiaries while they are still living so that they can see the gift being enjoyed. If you were to sell the funds with the large, unrealized gains to make that cash gift, then you would have to pay taxes on the gains. However, if you were to wait and bequeath those holdings with the large unrealized gains upon your death, your beneficiary would be able to benefit from a "step-up" in basis in your taxable brokerage account. Therefore, when your beneficiary goes to sell the funds, they will only pay taxes on gains since your date of death.

Another example of an asset to gift to children would be a Roth IRA. While the beneficiary will still need to take an annual required minimum distribution (RMD) from this Inherited Roth IRA, they won't have to pay taxes on withdraws like they would with a regular IRA or 401k. The Inherited Roth IRA will work very similar to how it did for the original owner prior to their death.

Why Leave an Inheritance?

Now that you have your estate plan in place and have chosen your beneficiaries, think about why you want to leave an inheritance.

> "A very rich person should leave their kids enough to do anything, but not enough to do nothing." —Warren Buffett

I've seen this quote in many different books and blogs, and for good reason. It seems to me exactly what we should do when it comes to planning for leaving an inheritance to our children and our children's children. We want them to be successful and have resources to fulfill their dreams, but we want them to build a life of their own.

An inheritance shouldn't enable them; it should ignite them. Igniting them to move forward with that business idea they have that will help improve the world. Igniting them to save for their children's college. Igniting them to be more generous with their time and resources and ultimately igniting them to create a plan to leave their children the same gift you were able to leave to them.

Let's discuss further the second half of that Warren Buffett quote: "but not enough to do nothing." When working with my clients, I often see one extreme or another when we discuss their desires to leave an inheritance to their children. One group wants to leave their children as much as possible, pay for their grandchildren's college, and gift to their children while they are still living. On the other hand, I also have clients who say they have worked hard their entire life and want to enjoy their money themselves, showing little interest in leaving an inheritance to their children. I even had one guy go as far to say that he wants to cross the finish line (referring to his death) just as he spends his last dime. Well, if we knew when we would die, then that would be easier to plan for!

Avoid Confrontation Amongst Beneficiaries

It seems like with an inheritance, we want to leave behind a legacy to our children and our children's children. From a financial standpoint, we want to be remembered for the way we took care of our finances and how we generously provided for our family.

What we don't want to be remembered for is causing our beneficiaries to fight and quarrel over the inheritance they received. So how do we prevent that? How to we keep our beneficiaries focused on the right things?

1. Let's go back to the Warren Buffett quote: "A very rich person should leave their kids enough to do anything, but not enough to do nothing." I bring this quote up again because it starts here. If you leave an inheritance of abundance that enables your beneficiaries to do nothing, then the inheritance will be idolized by them. The inheritance itself will become an idol, and they will fixate on the dollar amount itself and not on the opportunity you have bestowed upon them.

2. Discuss your plans with your family before your death. Be upfront about your desires for the inheritance you leave behind. Now, I'm not referring to restricting what the money can be used for and that kind of thing. I mean, *be clear* about who is to receive which account and who is to help initiate the desired distribution.

3. If you know that your children will not be the beneficiaries of an inheritance or that they will receive only a piece of your financial portfolio, then let this be known upfront. For

example, if you know that you will leave a large percentage to your church or your alma matter, then discuss this with your children. Otherwise, they may be falsely counting on that inheritance to supplement their retirement and will be in for a rude awakening when it comes time for them to inherit your wealth. Sharing your desires and reasons for leaving money to such an organization may also lead them to take interest in leaving something behind themselves. So not only would you be leaving a financial inheritance behind, but you could be passing on your generosity to your children and grandchildren.

CHAPTER 10

CLOSING: IMPLEMENTING A PLAN FOR YOUR FAMILY

As you can see, aligning your family values with your finances can be a complex endeavor with multiple moving pieces. So where do you start? I recently read a book by Gary Keller, *The One Thing*[28], and I've tried implementing the book's practices in my everyday life. A line that has stuck with me is "What's the one thing I can do such that by doing it everything else will be easier or unnecessary?" Then it gives examples of where to use this line of thinking, such as in your finances, relationships, spiritual life, health, job, business, and personal life.

What's the one thing that you really connected with in this book? What's the thing that you wrote down in your notes or told your spouse or a friend about?

Now that you have your "one thing," it's time to act. It's time to begin aligning your finances with your family values. This can't be done all at once and would be very overwhelming if attempted. Try implementing the topics from this book into your finances over a period of time, breaking these topics out by quarters. Over the next quarter of the year (the next three months) start with the most important "one thing." Then in the next quarter, implement a different topic.

For example, maybe you don't have an estate plan in place or have an outdated plan, this could be your "one thing." Over the next quarter, you should seek out an estate planning attorney to have an estate plan put in place. Once that is done, move on to the next category. Maybe you took away some tips on more efficient charitable gifting from this book and can begin implementing those.

Focusing on one thing at a time increases the likelihood that you will align your whole financial situation with your family values. Trying to do everything at once is more likely to overwhelm you and cause you to give up. This is like the people who set a New Year's resolution to lose weight. They either just set a blanket goal to lose weight or they may put a number on it like twenty-five pounds. When they start out with such a big goal, they may think, "How am I ever going to reach that goal?" Trying to accomplish this large goal all at once overwhelms them. While they may be on the right track, it doesn't feel that way, so they just give up. After a few weeks, they stop going to the gym on a regular basis because they're discouraged that they have only lost a fraction of the weight they are shooting for. And next year, their New Year's resolution is the same thing because they are still the same weight they were at the beginning of last year.

What if they rearranged the way they thought about their weight loss goal? What if instead of a general "lose twenty-five pounds goal," they set a goal to lose two pounds per month over the next year, which would put them very close to the twenty-five pounds goal? This incremental implementation, if accomplished each month, gradually accumulates. Fast-forward to next New Year's Day, and they are close to twenty-five pounds lighter! If they had stuck with the previous general twenty-five pounds weight loss goal, they would likely have given up.

This weight loss goal example is similar to the financial goal implementation, quarter by quarter. This way, you are more likely to achieve your goals over time versus getting overwhelmed and giving up on the ultimate goal of aligning your family values with your finances.

Now, a lot of these items won't take a full quarter to implement—some may take as little as twenty minutes, such as the case of updating your beneficiaries on your 401(k) account. If this is the case, you could make a list of multiple small things to focus on that quarter. For items that are more complex, such as the estate plan or establishing a workable budget that allows you to focus on items that are truly important to you, then you may need the whole quarter to implement them.

Parkinson's Law

This book has covered a lot of different issues. Changing your mindset, financial practices, and decisions to more closely align with your family values can be time-consuming and at times difficult. After all, these are potentially life-altering decisions that could impact your family for years to come. Therefore, I believe this actually *should* be a time-consuming process, but with a careful plan, it does not need to drag on endlessly.

This is where Parkinson's Law comes into play. Parkinson's Law is based on the premise that however much time you allow yourself to complete a task, that is how much time you'll use to complete that task. Therefore, if no plan is set in place to accomplish these tasks, then they will take much longer than needed. However, if you give yourself a reasonable deadline, you will be more inclined to complete the task. So, how do you go about implementing some of the actionable items from this book? Here is the game plan:

1. First, determine what stage of life you are in. If you are closing in on retirement, start with the topics we discussed in the Family & Retirement Planning chapter. If you are younger, consider the components of talking to your kids about money, setting up an estate plan, insurance policies, and overall budgeting to make sure you are on the right track.

2. Set calendar deadlines for each item. I've become a big proponent of chipping away at large goals over time. By this, I mean doing just a little bit each day or each week until over time you have accomplished something big! Often, if we try to accomplish the big goal all at once, we get overwhelmed and potentially give up by just putting it off, never actually doing it. For example, start budgeting by planning out your week every Sunday night. Consider how much you are going to spend on certain items and then execute that throughout the week. Over time, you will develop this habit and can pull back to doing this exercise once a month and then eventually once a quarter and so on.

3. Once you've set a plan to accomplish your primary goal, it is time to move on to the other aspects of your financial life. As previously mentioned, this is where you can implement the monthly or quarterly task schedule. This will help you stay on track, covering all financial areas of your life, and will prevent you from deviating from your ultimate goal.

Of course, these issues are not one-offs that never have to be revisited. While your initial planning is a good start, you must monitor these items on an ongoing basis, as your situation may change over time, as well as your desired goals.

I learned pretty early in my life that you can't do this alone. The weight of being the Chief Financial Officer of your family can be hard to carry. Getting support from your spouse or other members of your family is key. Even support from your friends or a professional team including a financial planner, accountant, and attorney will allow you to stay on track and achieve your ultimate goal.

To bring this book to a close, I want to share a story of how my family impacted my financial life. You see, I'm a financial planner by trade and spent a few years studying to become a CERTIFIED FINANCIAL PLANNER™. This wasn't an easy time in my life. The stress began to mount as I realized that in order to advance my career and to even potentially keep my job, I needed to study and pass this CFP exam.

As you will see, many sacrifices had to be made to achieve this goal. It didn't happen quickly, as I fell into the trap of "lose twenty-five pounds" versus "lose two pounds *per month*." With help from my family, I was able to dust myself off after failing to "lose those twenty-five pounds" quickly and ultimately was able to pass the exam by using the benefits it would provide my family as a motivator. However, this didn't come without struggles and unexpected turns along the way.

When Family Met Finance

I was working full-time at a local financial planning firm when I decided to spend about one and a half years going through N.C. State University's CERTIFIED FINANCIAL PLANNER™

Certification Program. Passing a program of this nature was required in order to sit for the CFP Exam. I did a combination of online courses as well as traditional classroom courses in order to complete each section of the certification program. Upon completion of the program in early 2015, I became eligible to register and sit for the CFP Exam.

Upon recommendation from my workplace family, I sought out a review course where I would travel to Charlotte, North Carolina and spend four days crammed in a classroom reviewing the ins and outs of specific trusts, life insurance policies, investment vehicles, retirement plans, and hundreds of other topics to best prepare myself to take the grueling exam.

I actually ended up taking two of these types of review courses in order to make sure I covered all the material. As you can imagine, these four days were long and tiresome. They wore me down, but I kept reminding myself that passing this exam would help me on my career path, and this would open doors for me and my family to be able to accomplish our goals and provide for our everyday needs.

Not only did I attend these review courses, but each one provided a stack of books that we were expected to read cover to cover in order to review for the test! Post review course, I had access to an online test bank of 2,500 questions, each of which

I completed multiple times. Huddled up in my "man room," I had a makeshift desk and a recliner where I spent hundreds of hours with my study buddy, Charlie. On top of a full-time job at a local financial planning firm, I had to come home to spend late hours studying for this exam. The exam caused me to miss anticipated sporting events, golf outings with friends, beach trips with my family, and general quality time with my wife in the hopes that passing the exam would help provide me with a defined successful future in my career.

I put everything I had into studying for this exam, and it showed. I was exhausted at work after regularly staying up past midnight studying for the exam. There were so many nights where my wife and couldn't even have dinner together because I was studying. I remember specifically going home to study the night of our third wedding anniversary. We went to dinner to celebrate, only for me to return home to a stack of books. This lifestyle seemed to take a toll on me, as I developed some stress-related health issues that I can only attribute to the process of preparing for this exam. As you can imagine, I was highly anticipating March 25, 2015, as this was the day I was scheduled to take the big exam.

My exam was at 11:00 a.m., and it was about a twenty-five to thirty-minute drive to the testing center. I had all the required materials: my HP 10bII financial calculator, my registration confirmation, and my driver's license to serve as my proof of documentation. I met my wife that morning at the local

Chick-fil-A to get a good luck Number One combo chicken biscuit and hash browns as a good luck charm. This go-to good luck charm ultimately served its purpose by the end of the day, but not without some major roadblocks along the way.

I arrived at my testing location at about 10:30 a.m. for my 11:00 a.m. exam. After checking in and putting my phone and keys in a locker, I took a quick bathroom break and was ready to go. The last thing you do before entering the testing room is verify your information, and they take a picture of you for security purposes. I was also prompted to provide my driver's license so it could be scanned, and this is where things got crazy. It turned out my license had expired just one month prior on my birthday, and this was a problem. The testing center was instructed that they could not let me sit for the exam with an expired license.

Panic began to set in. I saw the years of preparation and hundreds of hours of study flash before my eyes. I asked them what could I do and what were my options. There had to be something I could do, right?

Their resolution was that if I could get a new license or my passport by 11:30 a.m., I could take the exam. Keep in mind that at this point it was about 10:55 a.m., and I was thirty minutes away from home, so even if I had a passport (which I didn't), there was no way to go home to get it in time. So I went out to my car to regroup and figure out how to get a new license.

I pulled out my smartphone and frantically started searching online for a local DMV where I could renew my license. Lo and behold, there was a DMV just about two miles down the road. While that was great news, I couldn't help but think, "There is no way I can drive to the DMV, successfully renew my license, and drive back to the testing center in thirty-five minutes." Despite the minimal chances of accomplishing this, I fired up my Tacoma pickup and drove down to the DMV.

You know the drill. I checked in at the front door, was given a number, and waited in line until my number was called to meet with someone. Surprisingly, I was calm as I sat there waiting in a line about 10 people deep, which was strange, given how crazy the situation was and how much was on the line. For some reason, I decided at this time to text my wife and give her a heads up of what was going on. Here is the actual text message exchange I had with her as I sat in the DMV.

> Me: My driver's license expired. . . . Currently at DMV. If I get back by 11:30 I can take test today. . . . Ha. Can't make this stuff up!

> Abby: Cameron, are you joking? Are you there? What happens now? You have to be joking.

> Me: I'm sorry. . . . I don't know what happens if I don't get back in time. . . . I was so caught up in studying I didn't think about [my] license expiring.

Abby: Is there a line?

Is it close?

Me: My # is 2 away. So it will be close.

Abby: Let me know.

Is it close to testing center?

Cam, call me when you leave.

At this moment, I wasn't responding to her texts because my number had been called. I rushed up to the counter and took my signs and vision test and was then asked to pay the fee to renew the license. No problem, right? I handed over my debit card as quickly as I could and was ready to go. There was another problem, though—one that I wasn't prepared for.

Apparently, the DMV only accepted payments in cash, and I didn't have enough cash on hand to pay the full amount. Who knew this would be a problem in 2015!? I told the guy I didn't have the cash and asked what I could do. He said there was an ATM around the corner and I could go outside to use it.

I rushed outside looking for this ATM like it was a pot of gold at the end of a rainbow. But just like a pot of gold at the end of the rainbow . . . there was no ATM to be found. Starting to panic a little at this point, I looked around with my hands on my hips looking for a sign or help or something! Across the street, I saw what I was looking for. There was a corner gas station. I took off running toward it. There had to be an ATM in there, right? Thankfully, there was an ATM inside, and I fumbled through my wallet to get my debit card inserted into the slot. Warning signs popped up saying I would be charged a maintenance fee to use the ATM. . . . They could have charged me one hundred dollars and I still would have paid it at that point, I was so desperate. It spat out the cash and my receipt, and I took off running back towards the DMV.

At this point, I had no idea what time it was and had no time to stop and check. Entering the DMV, I bypassed the original numbered line and went straight towards my guy. He was, of course, helping a new customer by this point, but I had no time to wait. I threw my cash on the table and told him to keep the change as I went to the booth next to him to have my picture taken for my new license.

Imagining how my picture was going to turn out, I actually started laughing to myself. Here I was, visibly sweaty from running across a parking lot and the road to a gas station like a crazy person. I was given a quick printout of my temporary license and told to check it over for accuracy. Yeah, right. . . . I grabbed that piece of paper like it was the golden ticket to Willy Wonka's Chocolate Factory and took off towards my truck.

At this point, I knew my wife was a nervous wreck back at the house, so I gave her a quick call to update her. With the clock on my dash reading 11:24, I thought to myself: "I'm actually going to make it back in time. This is going to work!"

As I talked to my hysterically crying wife, I told her that everything was going to be fine and I was actually pretty pumped up at this point to take the exam. I guess the adrenaline rush of the previous thirty minutes was kicking into overdrive at this point. I told her that this was all just going to be a crazy story that I would tell later in life, and we would be sitting back and laughing about it a year from now.

I pulled into the testing center and walked through the door at 11:29 with a whole minute to spare. True to their word, they let me into the testing room with my newly acquired temporary license to begin my exam, heart beating out of my chest. The proctor asked me if I was okay, and I was able to mutter out that I was as I was trying to catch my breath. Thankfully, the exam had about ten minutes of intro material to give you got a chance to figure out how the software worked. This took me only about two minutes to complete, but probably my best strategic move of the day was sitting there for the entire ten minutes before clicking "done" to give myself time to catch my breath.

A marathon of testing ensued, and I proceeded to pour everything I had left into that exam. All the long study hours, review courses, the crazy thirty minutes at the DMV—all went into this moment. I was finally answering questions about the material that I knew I knew and was eager to figure out the best answers to benefit the case study clients I was given. Taking up the whole allotted time for the exam, I was finally greeted with a screen telling me I had finished.

It was over. Hundreds of questions answered and hours had gone by. Taking a deep breath, I clicked submit. . . . "Congra—" was all I saw on the next page before I threw my hands up in the air with a big exhale. I passed! It was finished! I was so excited but too tired to even show it! I just leaned back and smiled.

I then stumbled out to my truck in exhaustion. I got my phone out to call my wife and other family members to share the good news when I noticed I had an unread message from my wife:

> Called out the troops to pray for you, boo. Praying on my knees for you, for God to give you his peace and feel his presence in this. For Him to guide you to the right answers. For Him to allow you to pass and become a CFP and use the certification for his glory and this story for his glory. God obviously was in this, no way you could have made it to the DMV and back in time without Him. Love you, Cam. We all will be praying for you all day!

Looking back at this day, I realize I couldn't have done it without the support I received from my wife and family. Through it all, my wife supported and encouraged me along the way. The text messages from her show how deeply involved and in-grained in the process she was. It was the truest combination of family and finances that I have seen.

Financial planning has been a passion of mine for a while now, and seeing the support from my wife as well as other family members throughout the whole process showed me the im-portance of each. It validated my desire to become a finan-cial planner and to eventually write this book about family and finances.

The funny thing is, we did get to laugh about this wild story a year later. Remember the story I told you about my dog and picking him up from the three-week board and train program? The day we picked him up was March 25, 2016, a year to the day from my CFP exam. A year to the day from one of the most unbelievable experiences of my life and one that I told my wife we would be laughing about a year later. A year to the day was when I decided I was going to embark on this book writing journey. I knew that the book had to involve family and finances somehow.

Family and finance met for me during this journey, and now I got to interlock the two for you through this book.

Sticking with the theme of this book, the reason you are focus-ing on these financial areas is to ultimately benefit your family.

You can read all the personal finance books out there, but at the end of the day, it's up to you to act. I can give you useful tips or inspiration to take action, but as Clemson head football coach Dabo Swinney said, "I can't give you guts, and I can't give you heart. You got to B.Y.O.G." (Bring Your Own Guts).[29]

1. bwatson. (2017, April 1). *7 Common Conflict Issues in Marriage*. Retrieved from Directed Path Ministries: http://www.directedpathministries.com/907/

2. Ramsey, D. (2015). *Financial Peace University*.

3. Vanguard. (2014). *The added value of financial advisors*.

4. Matthew. (2017, April 1). *Parable of the Three Servants*. Retrieved from Bible Gateway: https://www.biblegateway.com/passage/?search=Matthew+25%3A14-30&version=NLT

5. Brown, A. (2017, April 1). *When Is a Penny Worth More Than A Million-Dollar Check?* Retrieved from Forbes: https://www.forbes.com/sites/abrambrown/2012/09/10/which-would-you-chose-1-million-today-or-10-7-million-in-a-month/#188b61527693

6. Vanguard. (2016, April 1). *The global case for strategic asset allocation and an examination of home bias*. Retrieved from https://advisors.vanguard.com/iwe/pdf/ISGGAA.pdf?cbdForceDomain=true

7. Davis Advisors. (2016, April 1).

8. Morningstar. (2016, April 1). *Mind the Gap 2014.* Retrieved from http://www.morningstar.com/advisor/t/88015528/mind-the-gap-2014.htm

9. Vanguard. (2014). *The added value of financial advisors.*

10. Hicken, M. (2017, April 1). *Workes spend more time planning vacation than retirement.* Retrieved from CNN: http://money.cnn.com/2014/08/19/retirement/401k-investments/

11. Schmalbruch, S. (2017, April 1). *Some of the most Successful Businessess In The US Were Started By Entrepreneurs Over Age 50.* Retrieved from Business Insider: http://www.businessinsider.com/entrepreneurs-over-50-2014-

12. Anthony, M., & Sanduski, S. (2016, April 1). *Retirement Coaching Training Program.*

13. Anthony, M., & Sanduski, S. (2016, April 1). *Retirement Coaching Training Program.*

14. Anthony, M., & Sanduski, S. (2016, April 1). *Retirement Coaching Training Program.*

15. Anthony, M., & Sanduski, S. (2016, April 1). *Retirement Coaching Training Program.*

16. Merrill Lynch. (2016). *Age Wave.*

17. Anthony, M., & Sanduski, S. (2016, April 1). *Retirement Coaching Training Program.*

18. Onink, T. (2017, April 1). *College Is A Toll Booth On The Road To Retirement.* Retrieved from Forbes: https://www.forbes.com/sites/troyonink/2012/03/12/college-is-a-toll-booth-on-the-road-to-retirement/#431ca58a57c5

19. ESPN. (2017, April 1). *Life on the lake with Nick Saban.* Retrieved from ESPN: http://www.espn.com/video/clip?id=17383517

20. Hero, S. L. (2016). *Student Loan Debt Statistics.* Retrieved from Student Loan Hero: https://studentloanhero.com/student-loan-debt-statistics/

21. NCF. (2016). *Plan to Give Conference.* Retrieved from Plan To Give NC: http://plantogivenc.com/

22. Wells Fargo. (2017, April 1). *Conversations about personal finance more difficult than religion and politics.* Retrieved from Wells Fargo: https://www.wellsfargo.com/about/press/2014/20140220_financial-health/

23. T. Rowe Price. (2017, April 1). *8th Annual Parents, Kids & Money Survey.* Retrieved from T.Rowe Price: https://

corporate.troweprice.com/Money-Confident-Kids/ images/emk/2016pkmresultsdeckfinal-160322181149.pdf

24. Disability Can Happen. (2017, April 1). *You, disabled? What are your chances?* Retrieved from Disability Can Happen: http://www.disabilitycanhappen.org/chances_disability/

25. Genworth. (2017, April 1). *Compar Long Term Care Costs Across the United States.* Retrieved from Genworth: https://www. genworth.com/about-us/industry-expertise/cost-of-care. html

26. Ramsey, D. (2016). *The Legacy Journey.* Ramsey Press.

27. *Proverbs 13:22.* (2017, April 1). Retrieved from BibleGateway: https://www.biblegateway.com/passage/?search=Proverbs +13%3A22&version=KJ21

28. Keller, G. W., & Papasan, J. (2016). *The ONE Thing.* Bard Press.

29. Swinney, D. (2015). Retrieved from byoggear: http://www. byoggear.com/

Made in the USA
Middletown, DE
19 May 2017